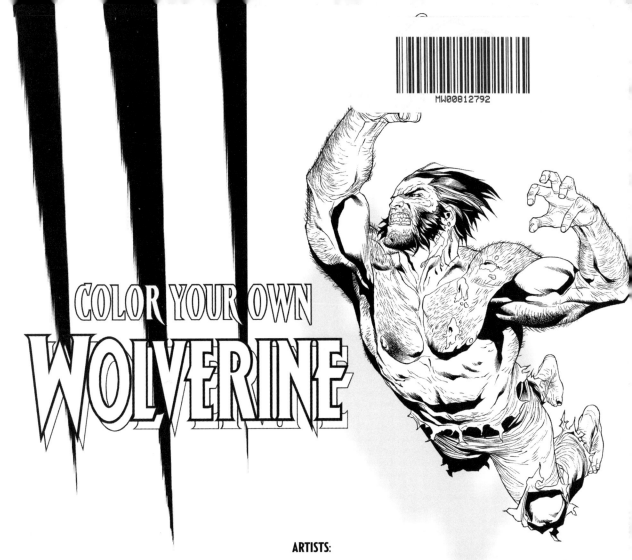

COLOR YOUR OWN WOLVERINE

ARTISTS:

Ed McGuinness, Dexter Vines, Mark Bagley, Andrew Hennessy, Mike Zeck, Joe Quesada, Mark Morales, Steve McNiven, Jay Leisten, Mario Del Pennino, Arthur Adams, Dave Cockrum, Gil Kane, Herb Trimpe, Jack Abel, Todd McFarlane, Bob Wiacek, Barry Windsor-Smith, Frank Cho, Phil Jimenez, John Romita Jr., Jim Lee, Scott Williams, Nick Bradshaw, John Buscema, Alan Davis, Mark Farmer, Klaus Janson, Ryan Stegman, Gerardo Sandoval, David Finch, Danny Miki, Philip Tan, Bryan Hitch, Paul Neary, Frank Miller, Joe Rubinstein, Al Williamson, Leinil Francis Yu, Stephen Segovia, Renato Guedes, José Wilson Magalhaes, Oclair Albert, Marc Silvestri, Dan Green, John Byrne, Terry Austin, Carlos Pacheco & Cam Smith

COLLECTION EDITOR: Jennifer Grünwald
ASSOCIATE MANAGING EDITOR: Kateri Woody
EDITOR, SPECIAL PROJECTS: Mark D. Beazley
VP PRODUCTION & SPECIAL PROJECTS: Jeff Youngquist
SVP PRINT, SALES & MARKETING: David Gabriel
RESEARCH: Jess Harold
BOOK DESIGNER: Jay Bowen

EDITOR IN CHIEF: Axel Alonso
CHIEF CREATIVE OFFICER: Joe Quesada
PUBLISHER: Dan Buckley
EXECUTIVE PRODUCER: Alan Fine

COLOR YOUR OWN WOLVERINE. First printing 2017. ISBN# 978-1-302-90384-8. Published by MARVEL WORLDWIDE, INC., a subsidiary of MARVEL ENTERTAINMENT, LLC. OFFICE OF PUBLICATION: 135 West 50th Street, New York, NY 10020. Copyright © 2017 MARVEL No similarity between any of the names, characters, persons, and/or institutions in this magazine with those of any living or dead person or institution is intended, and any such similarity which may exist is purely coincidental. **Printed in the U.S.A.** ALAN FINE, President, Marvel Entertainment; DAN BUCKLEY, President, TV, Publishing & Brand Management; JOE QUESADA, Chief Creative Officer; TOM BREVOORT, SVP of Publishing; DAVID BOGART, SVP of Business Affairs & Operations, Publishing & Partnership; C.B. CEBULSKI, VP of Brand Management & Development, Asia; DAVID GABRIEL, SVP of Sales & Marketing, Publishing; JEFF YOUNGQUIST, VP of Production & Special Projects; DAN CARR, Executive Director of Publishing Technology; ALEX MORALES, Director of Publishing Operations; SUSAN CRESPI, Production Manager; STAN LEE, Chairman Emeritus. For information regarding advertising in Marvel Comics or on Marvel.com, please contact Vit DeBellis, Integrated Sales Manager, at vdebellis@marvel.com. For Marvel subscription inquiries, please call 888-511-5480. **Manufactured between 12/2/2016 and 1/9/2017 by SHERIDAN, CHELSEA, MI, USA.**

10 9 8 7 6 5 4 3 2 1

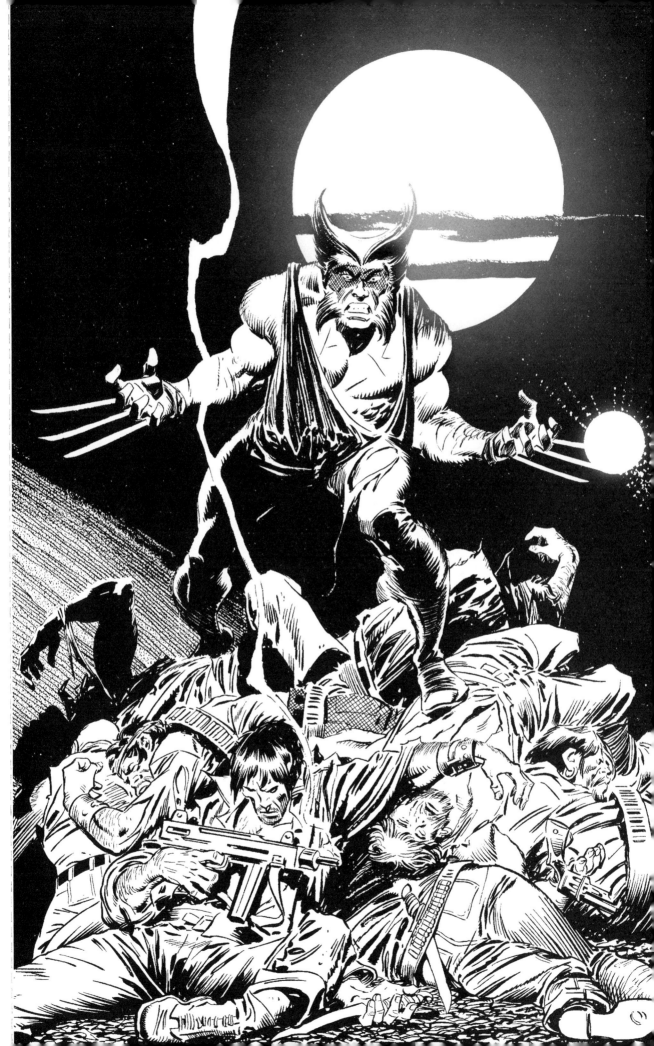

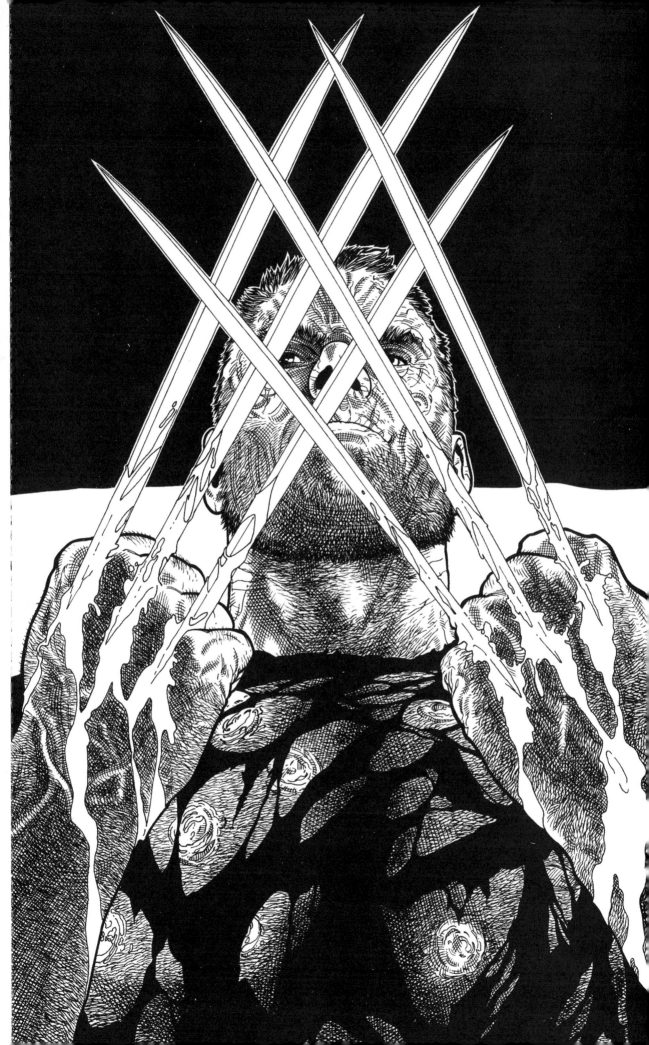

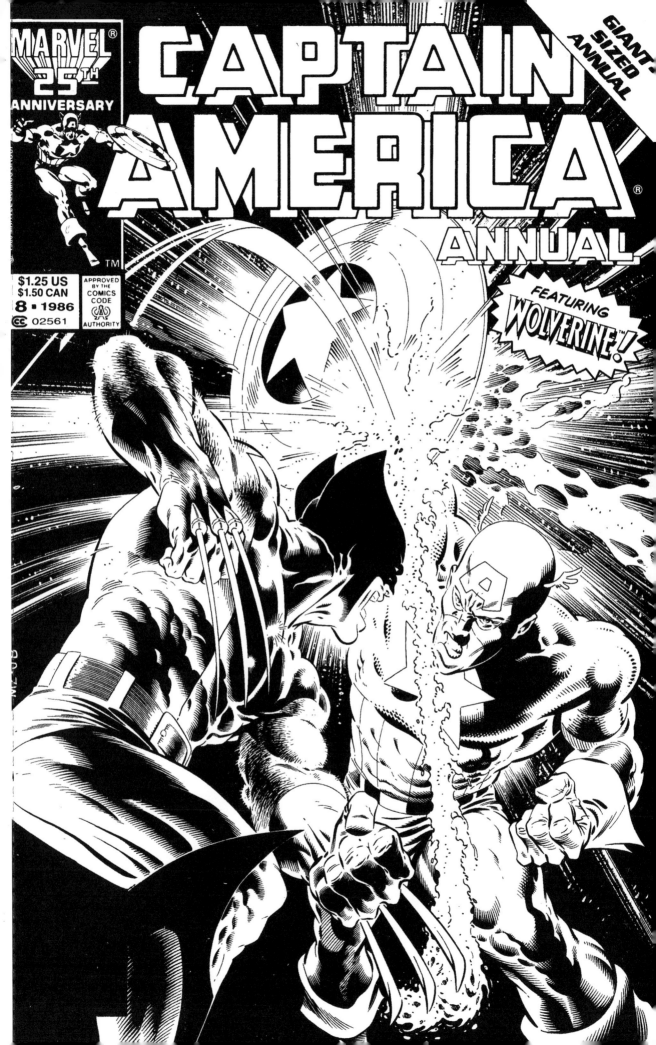

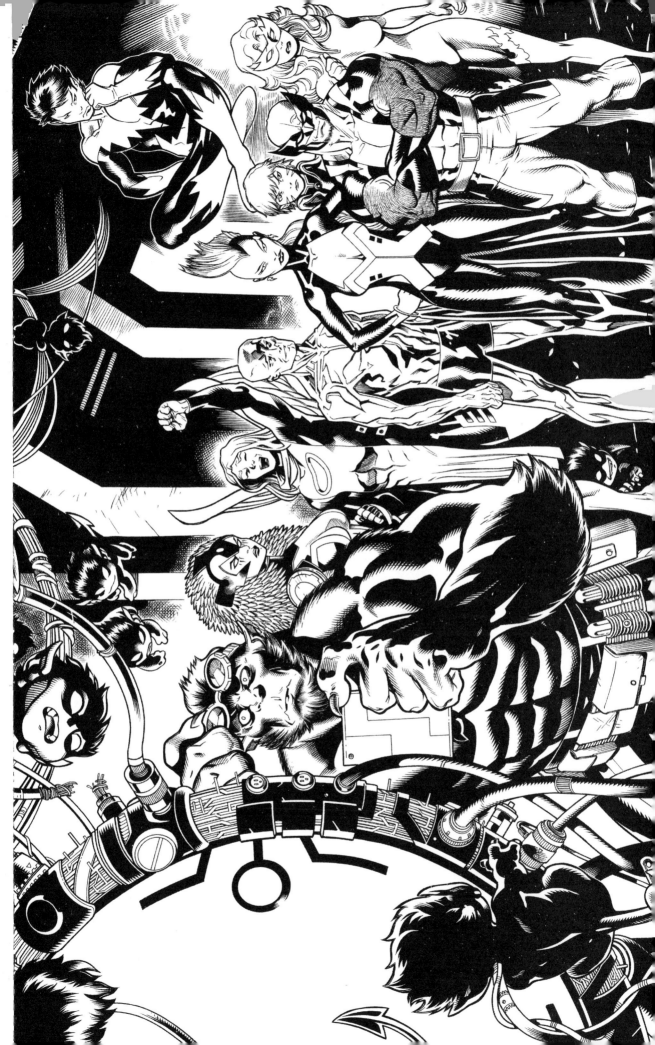

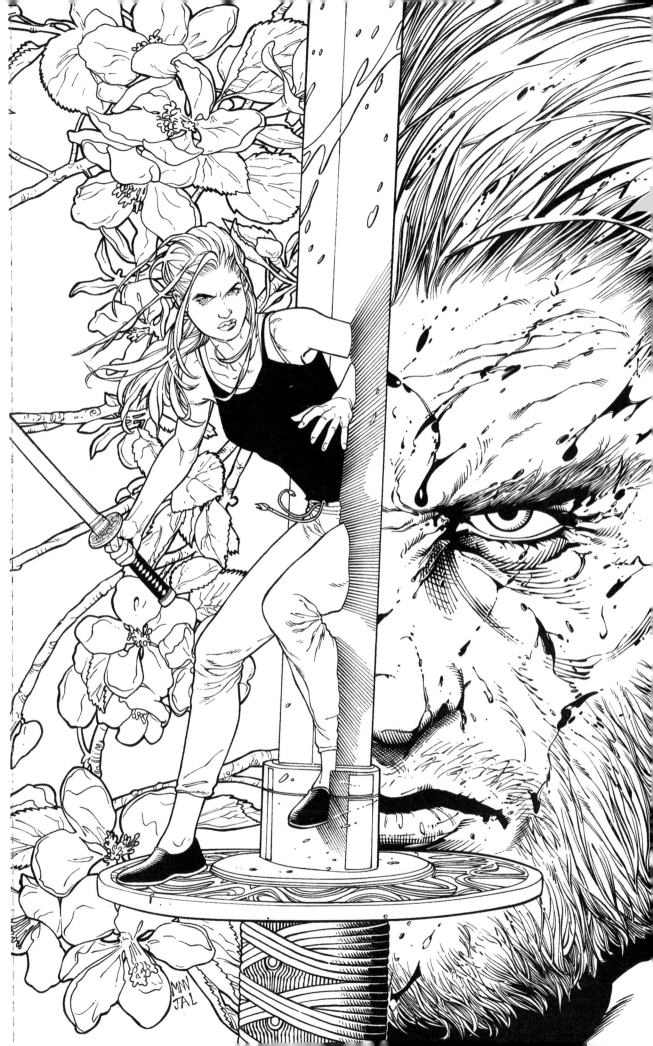

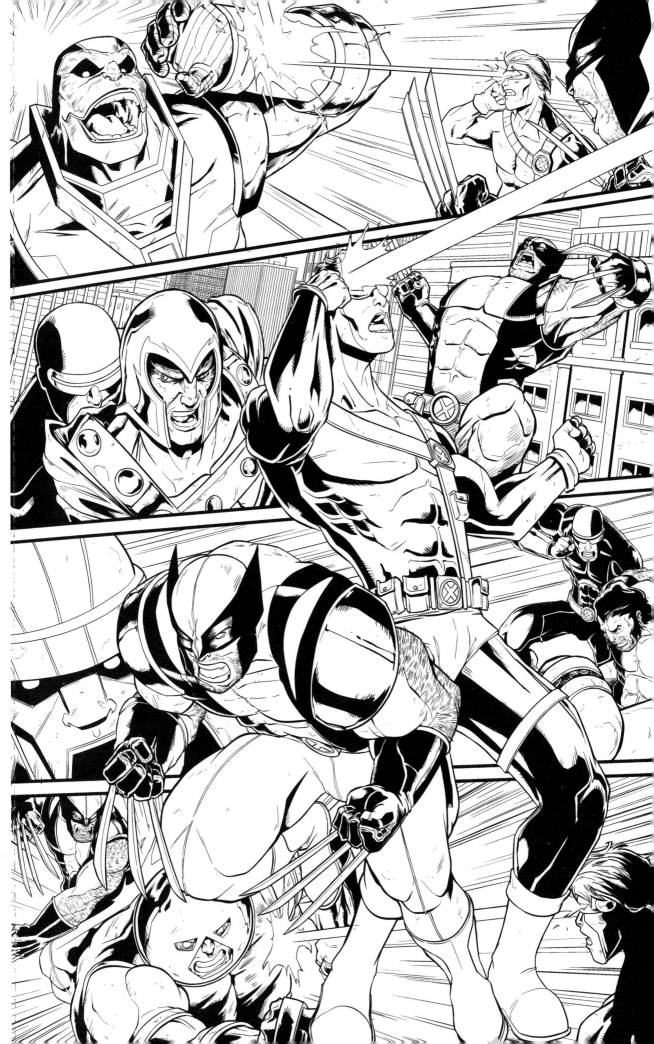

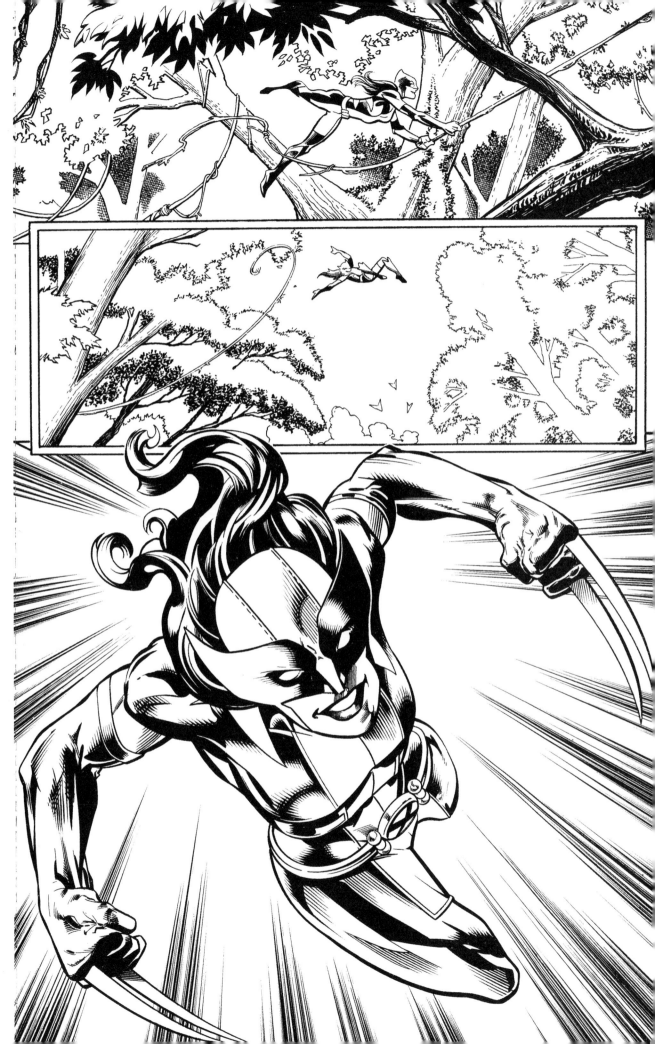

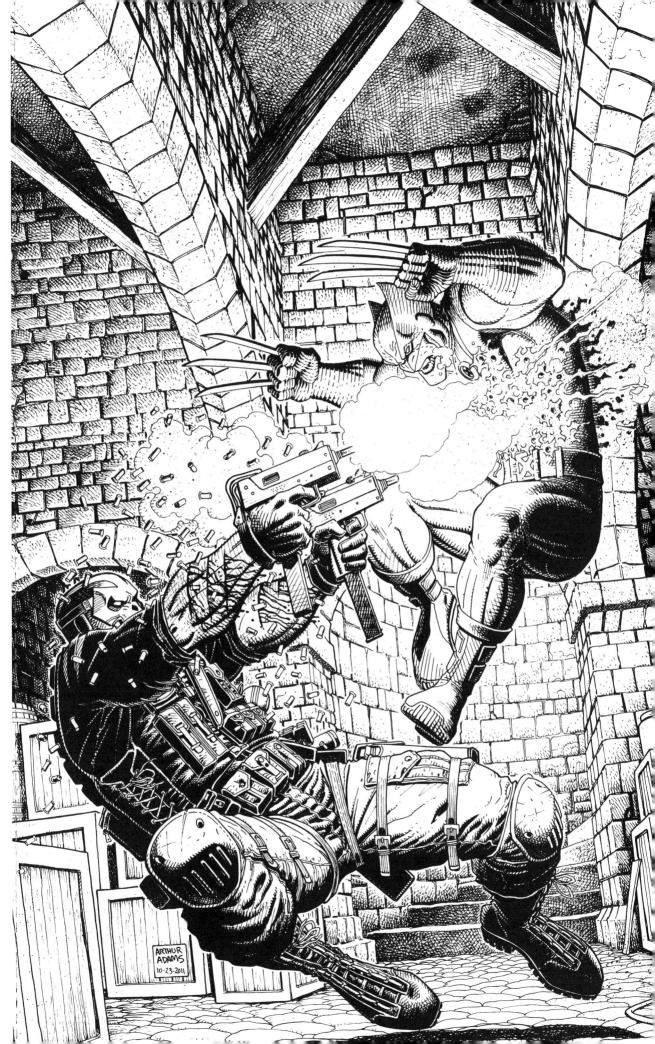

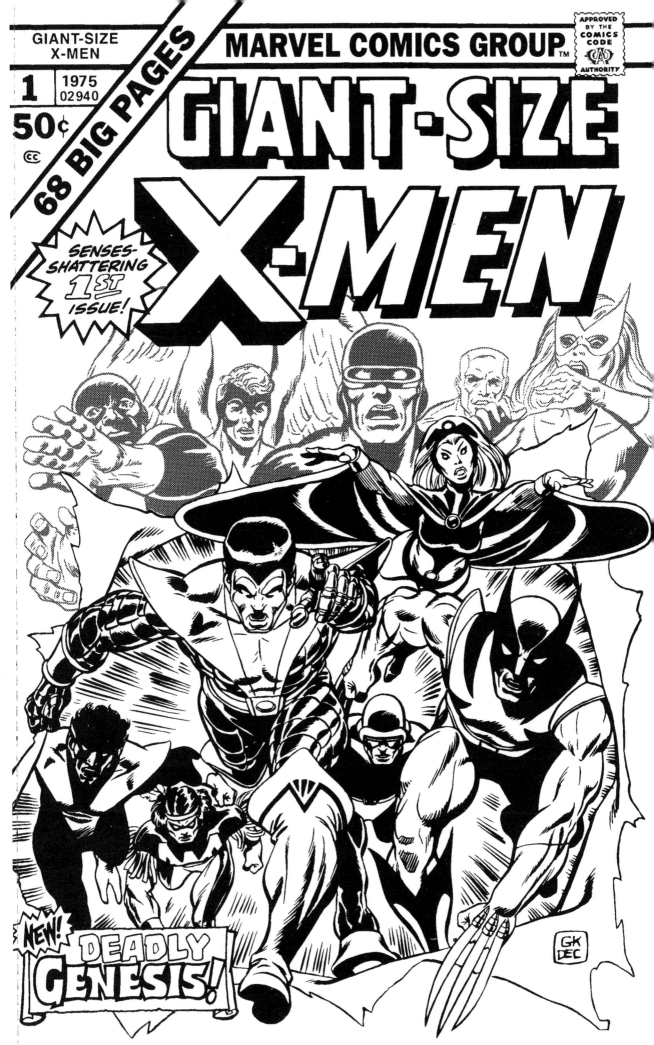

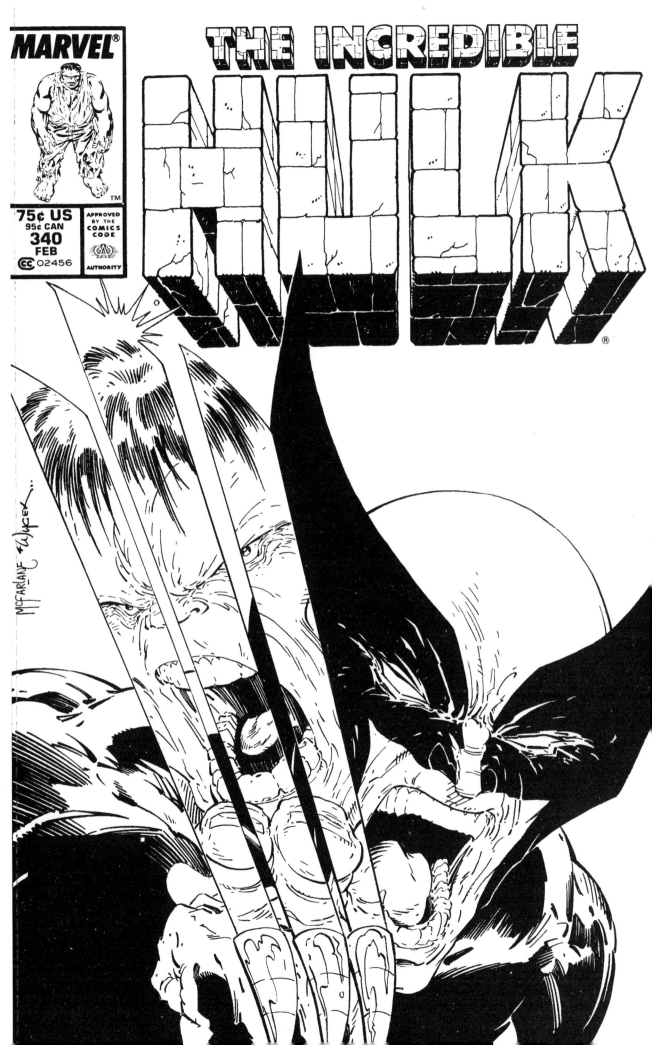

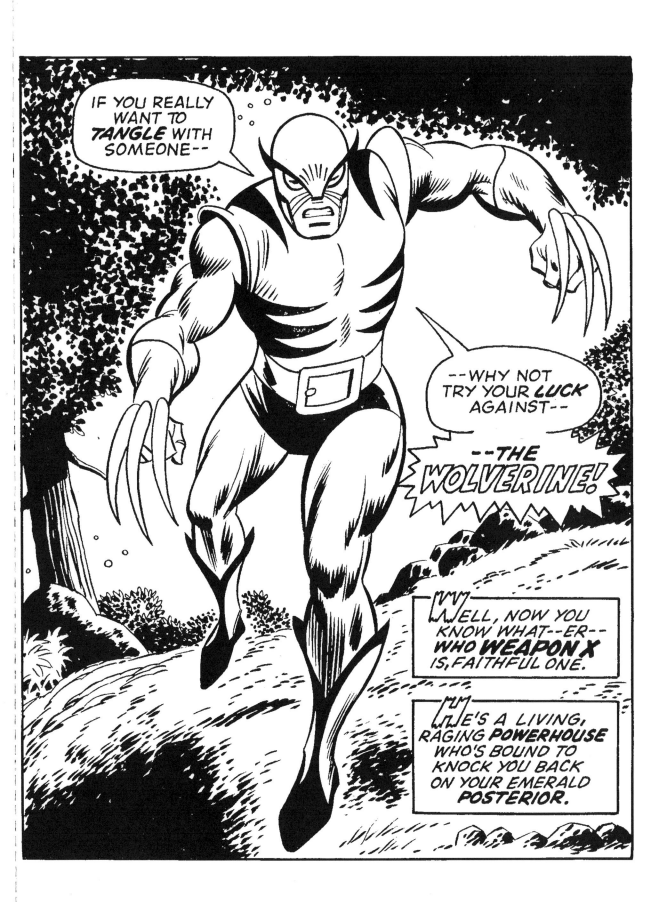

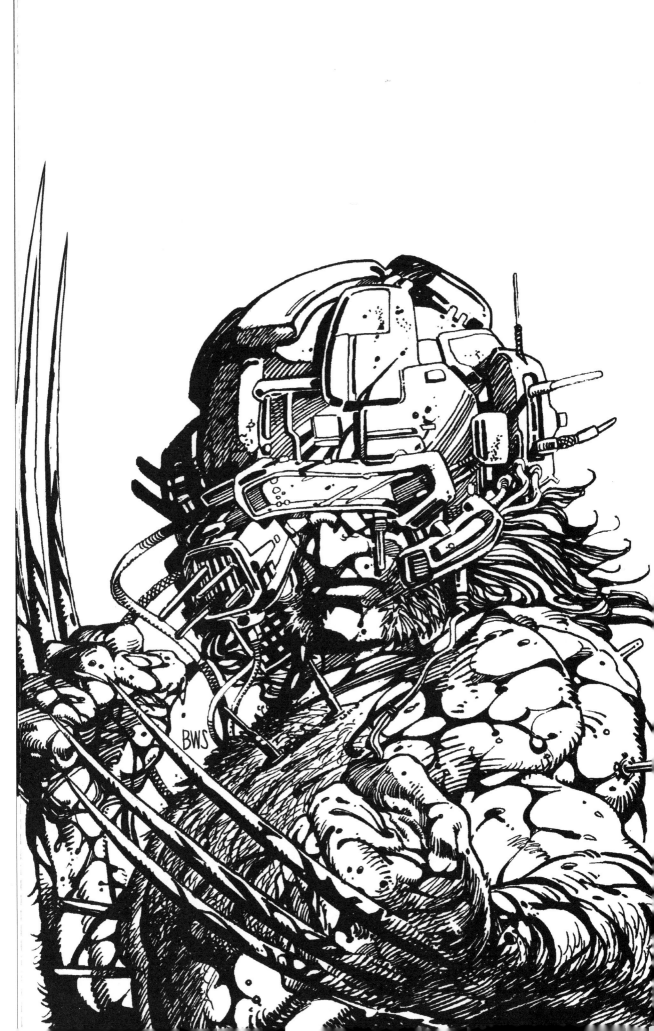

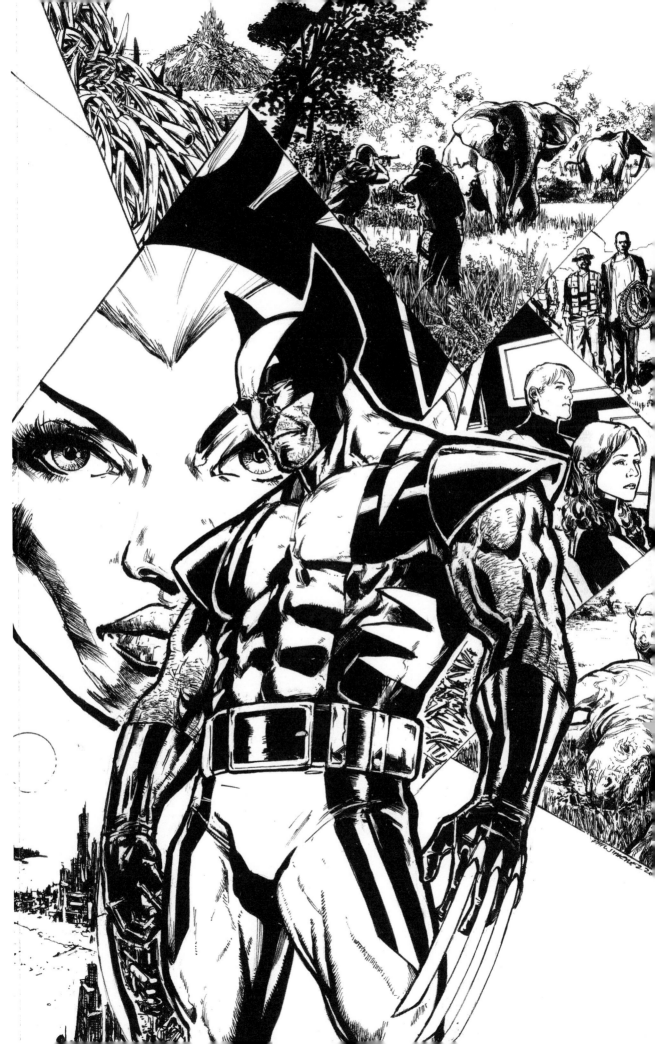

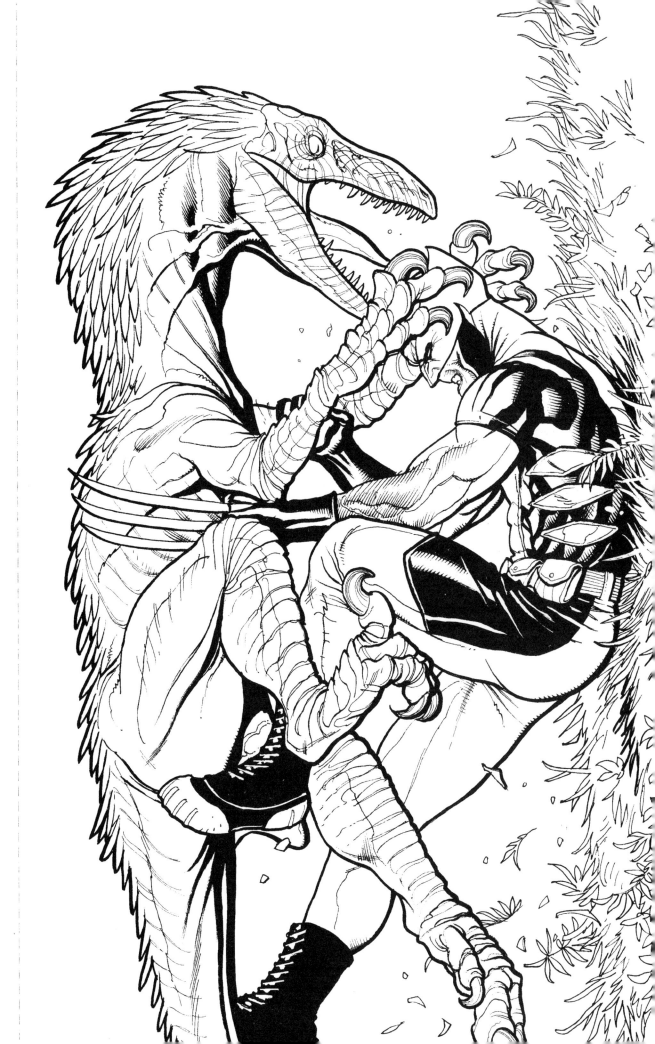

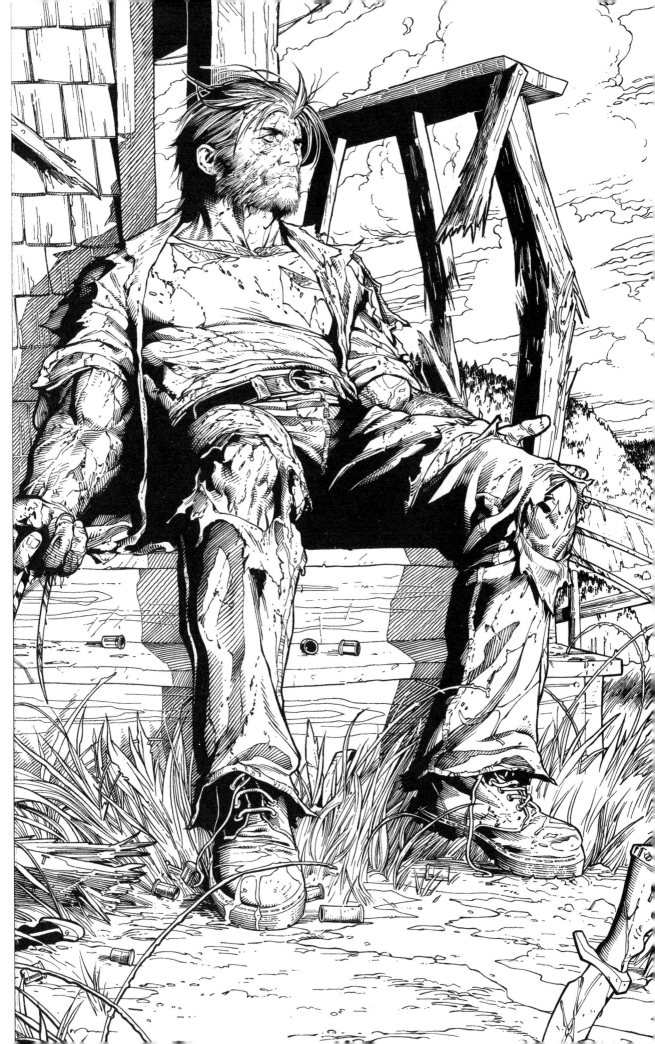

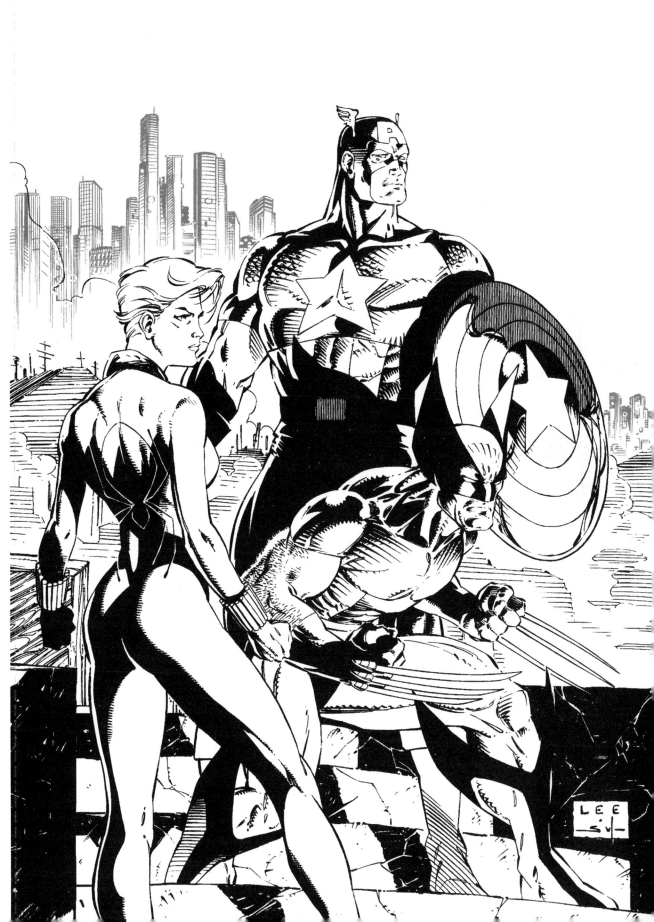

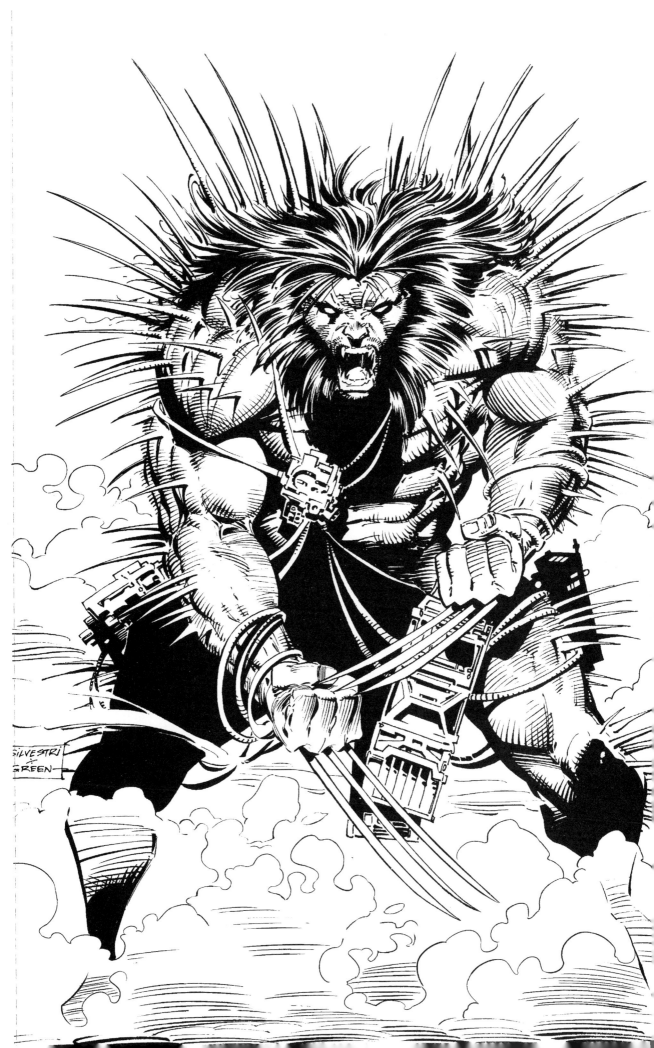

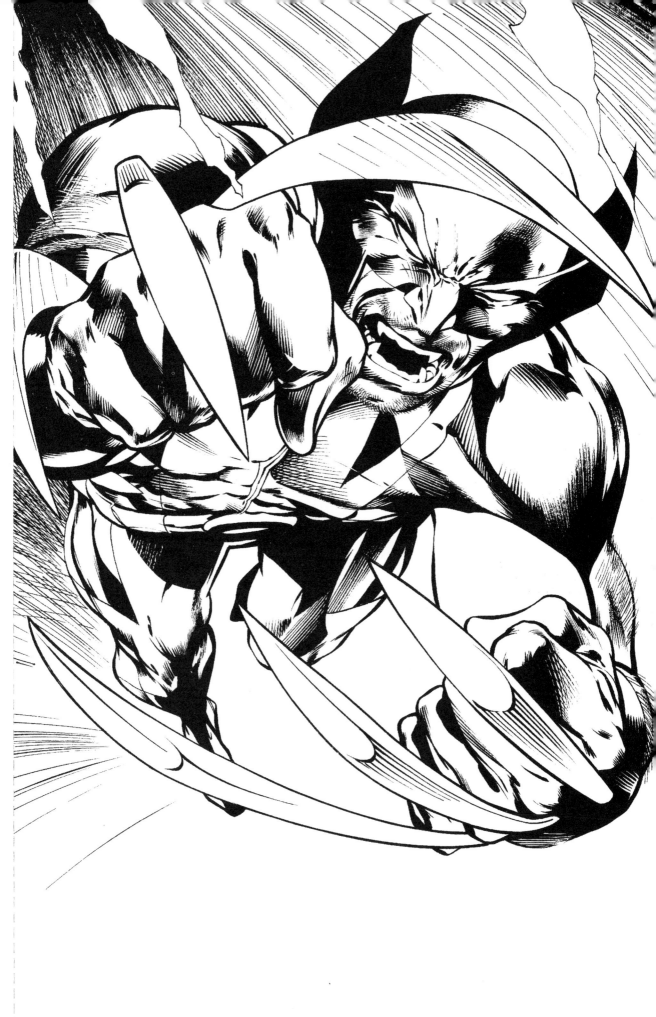

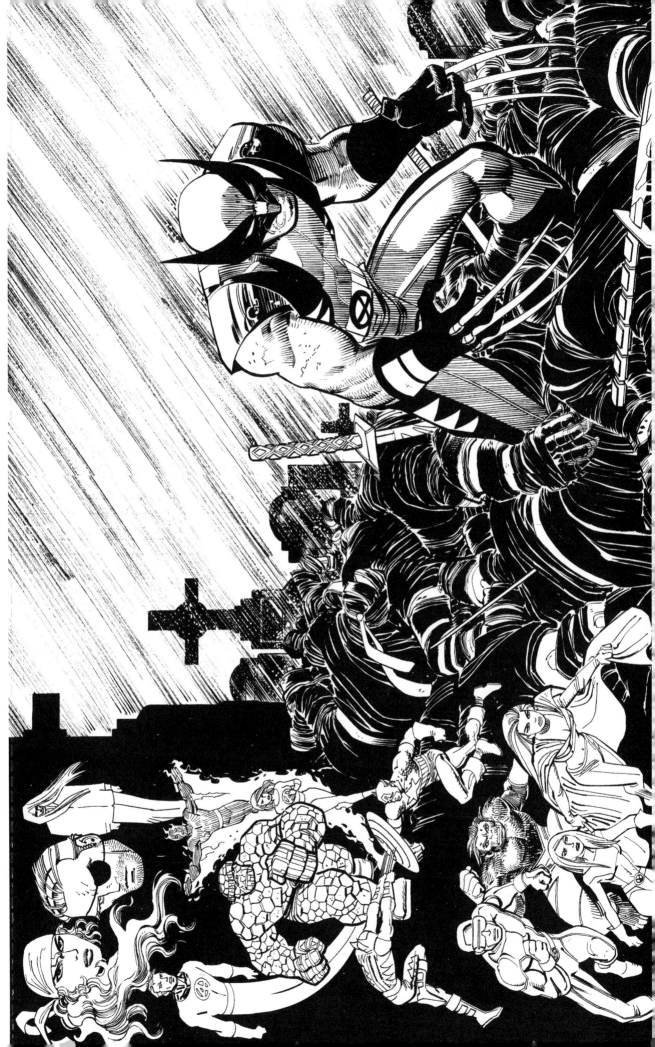

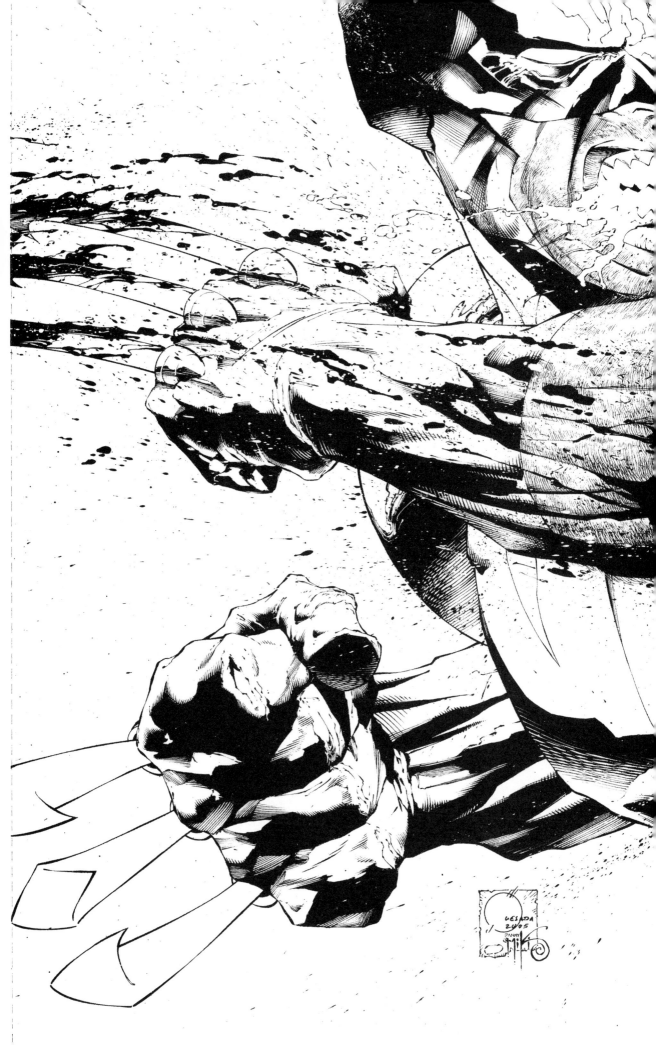

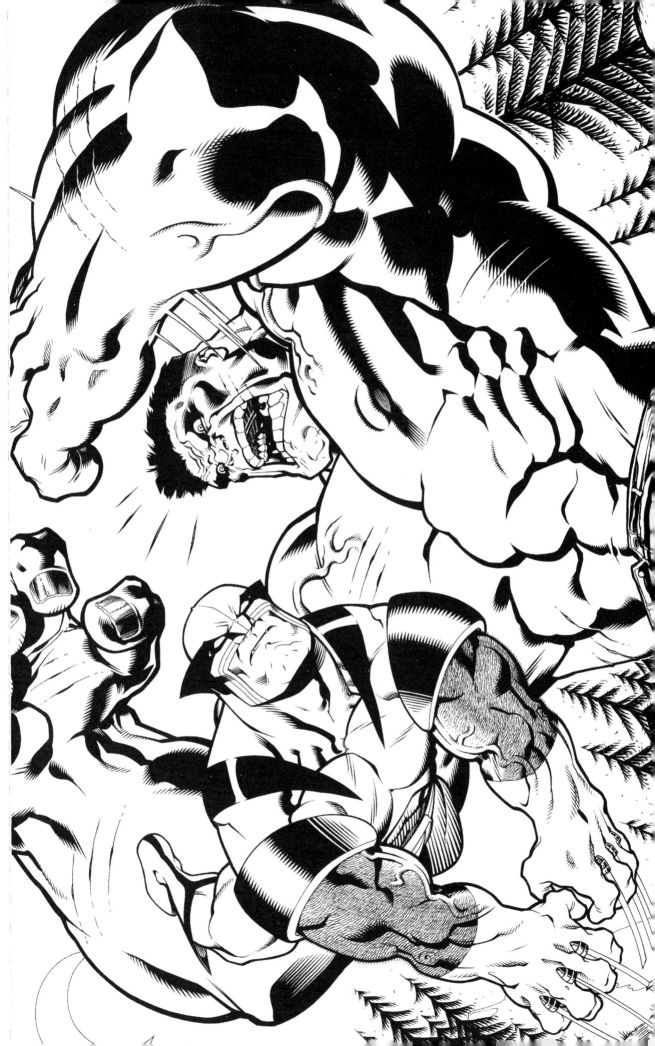

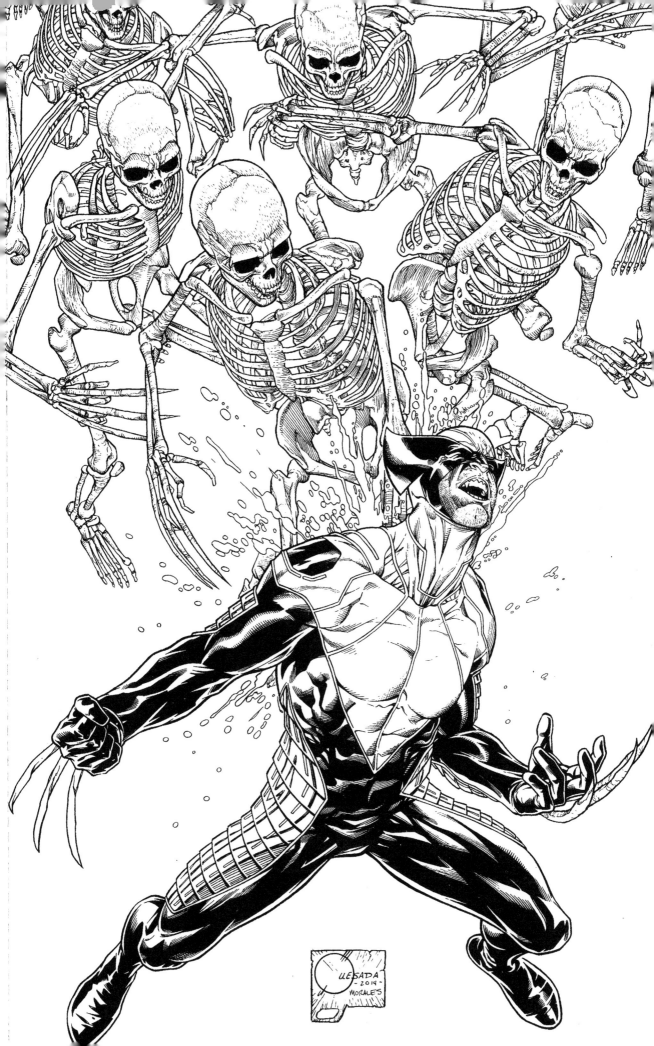

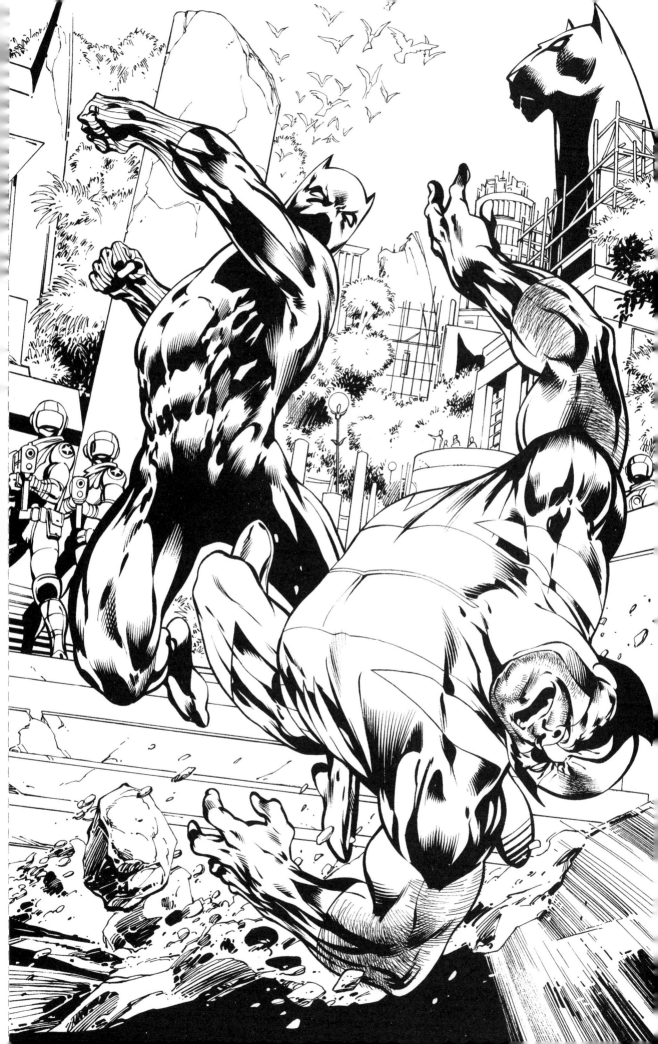

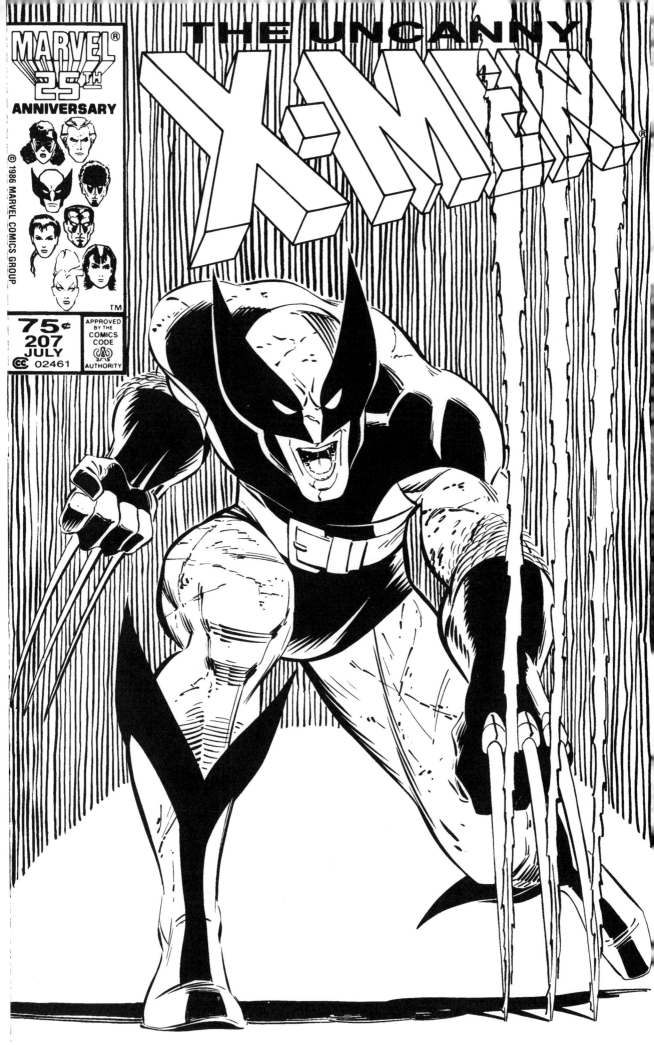

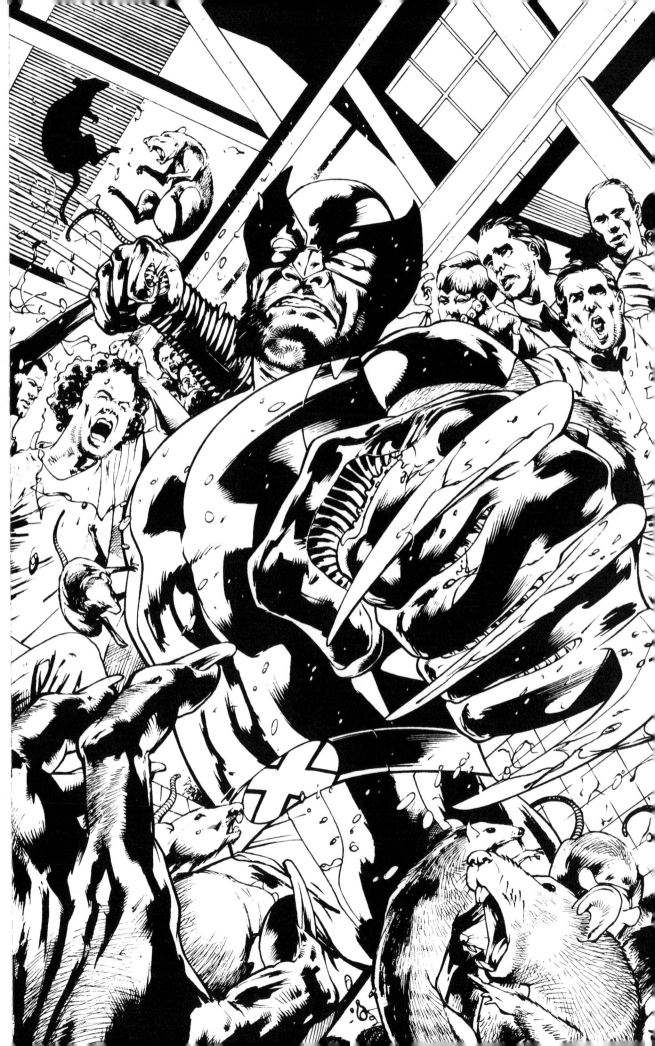

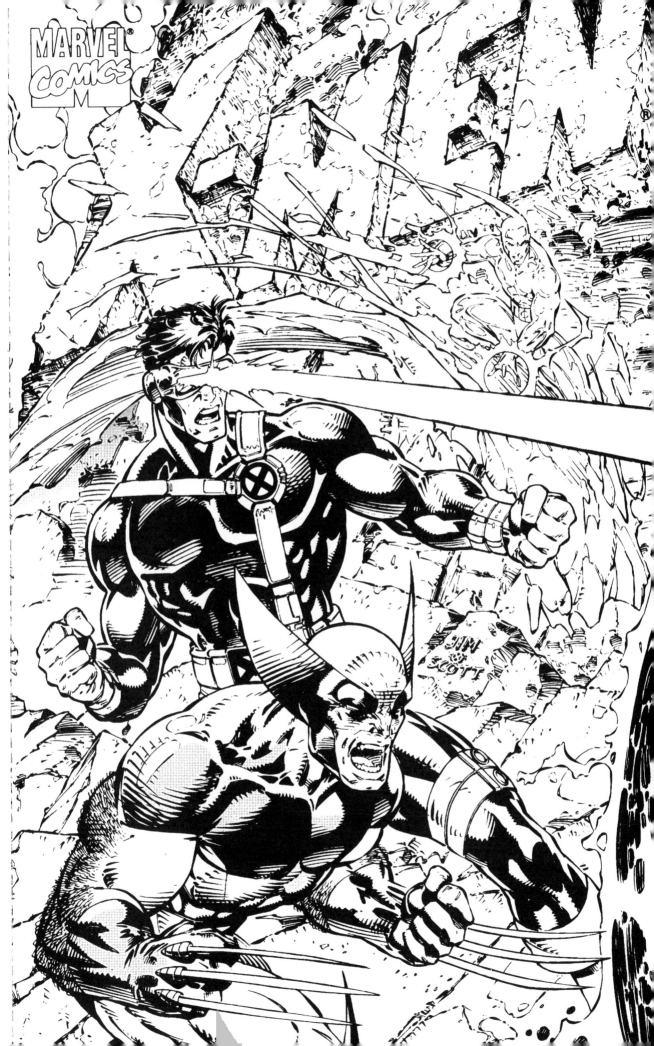

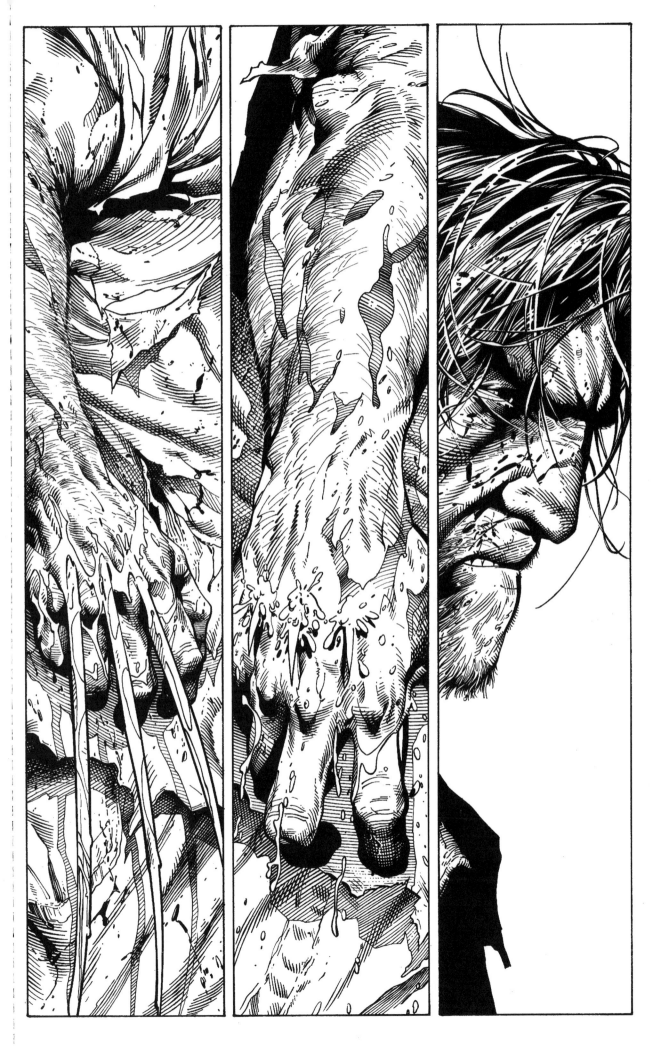

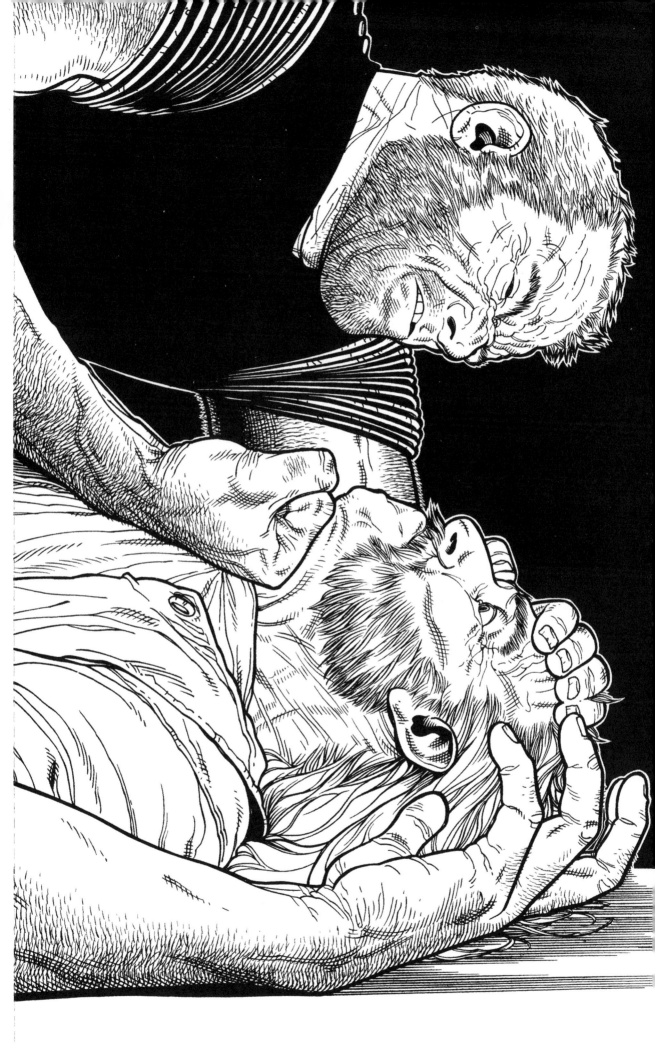

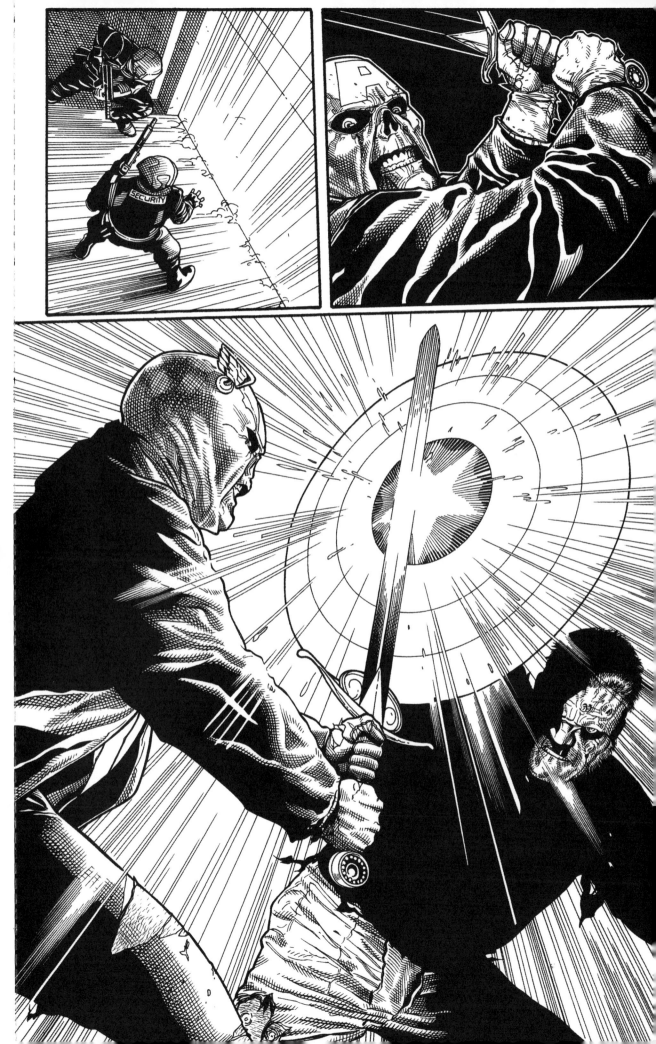

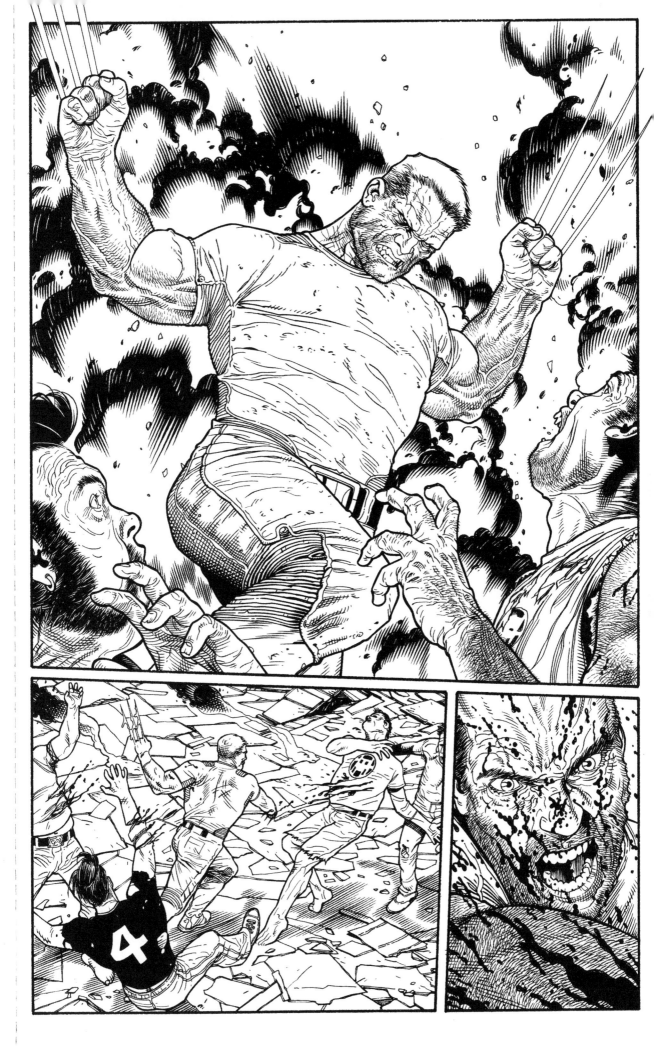

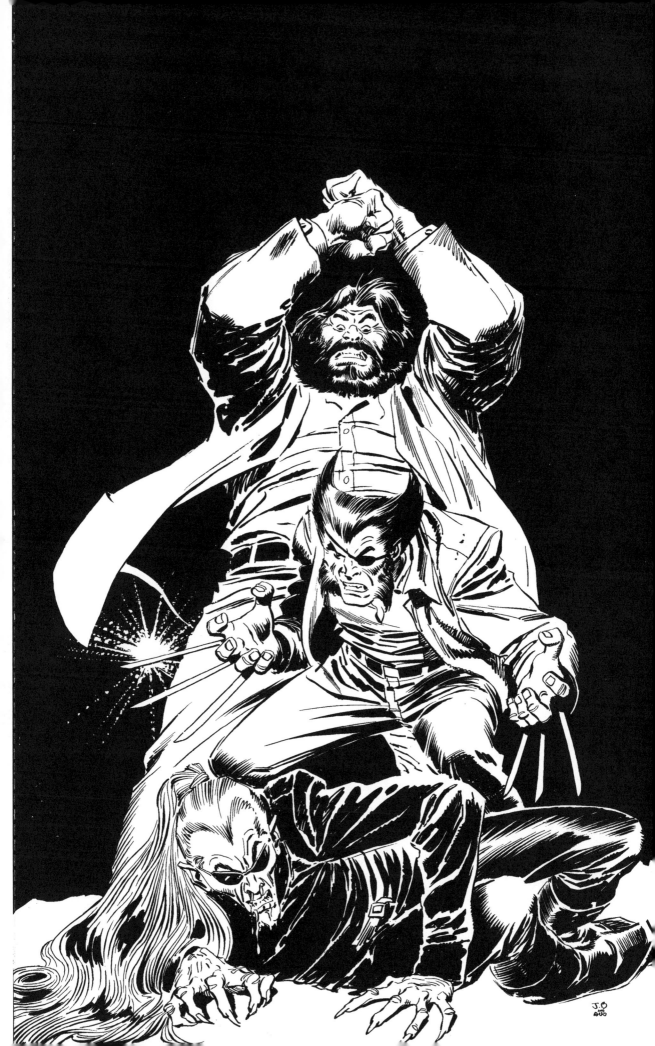

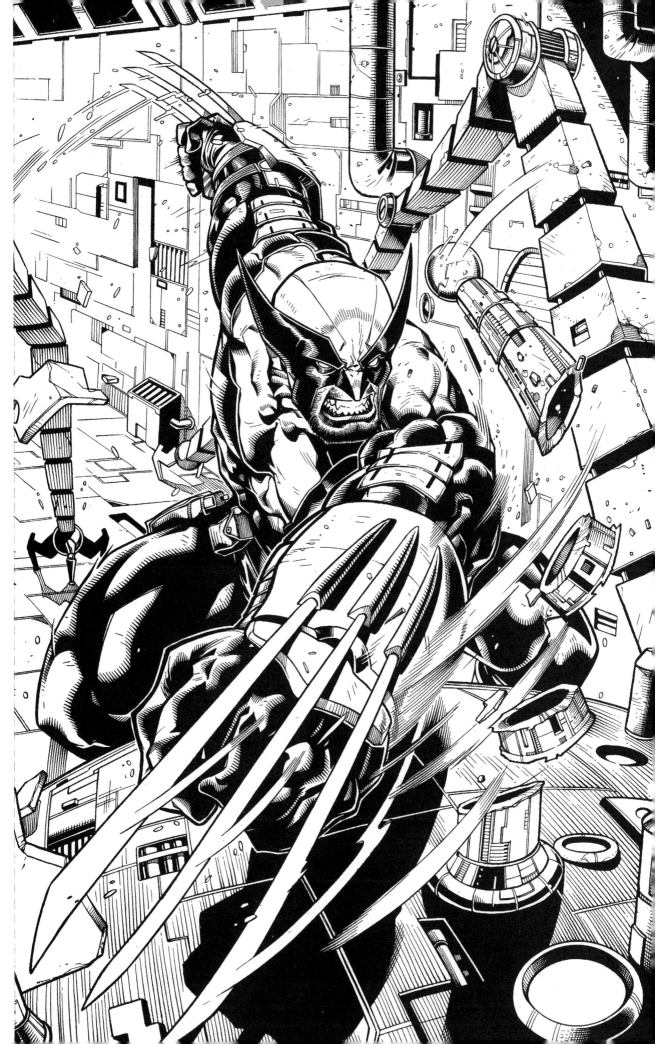

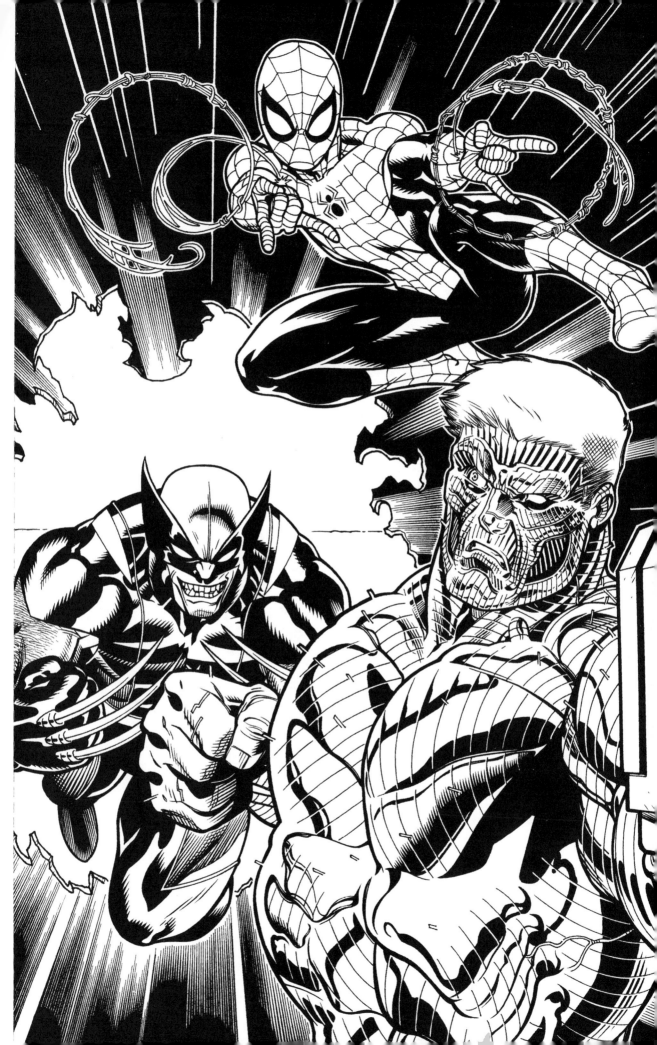

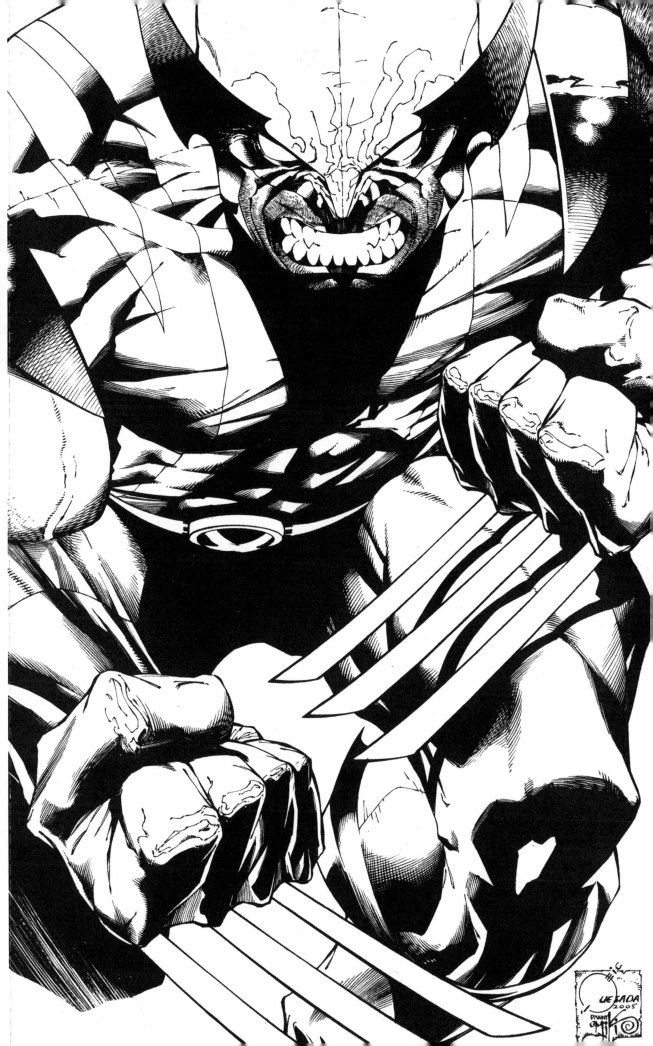

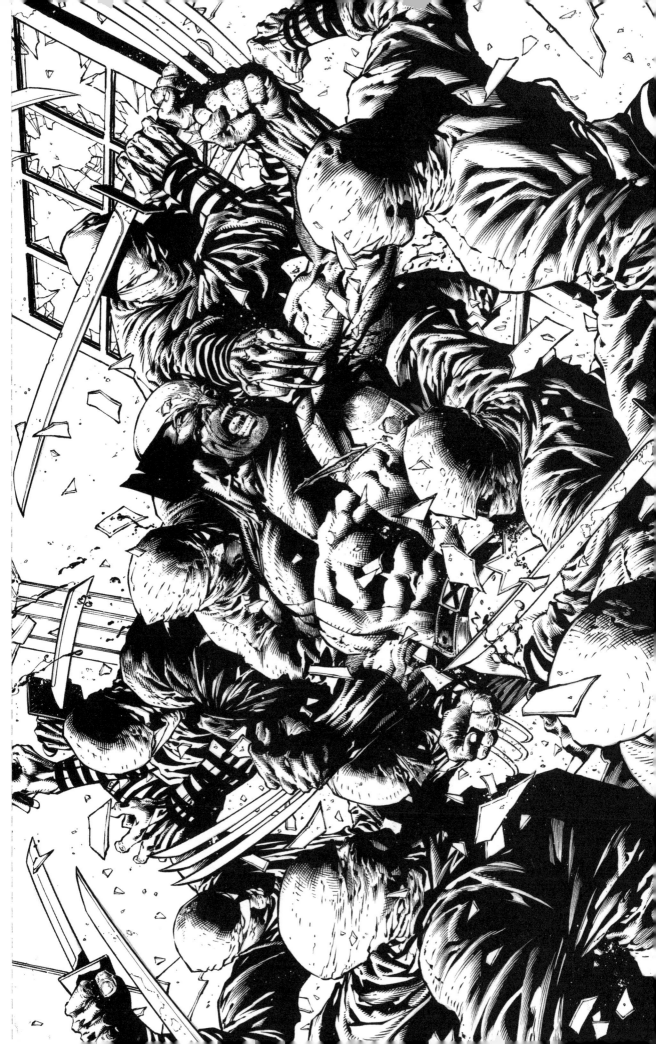

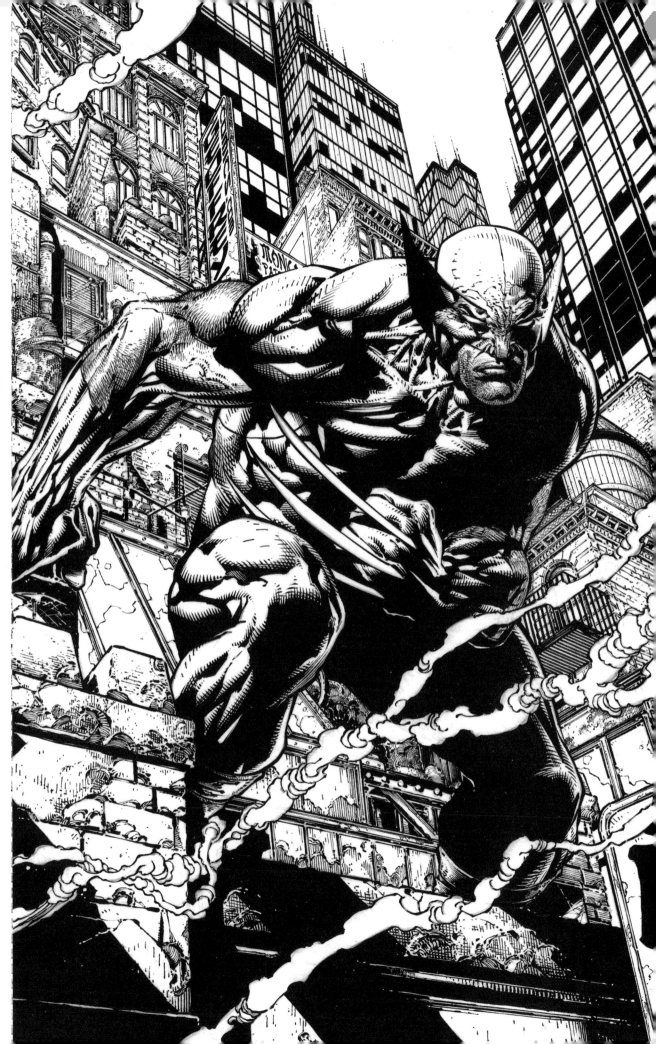

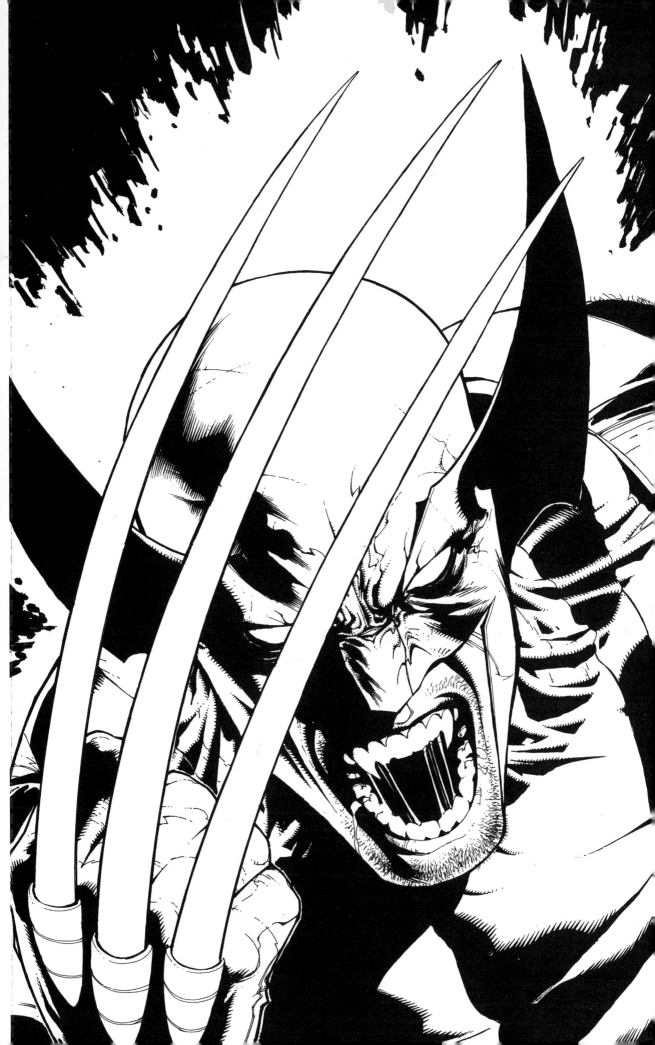

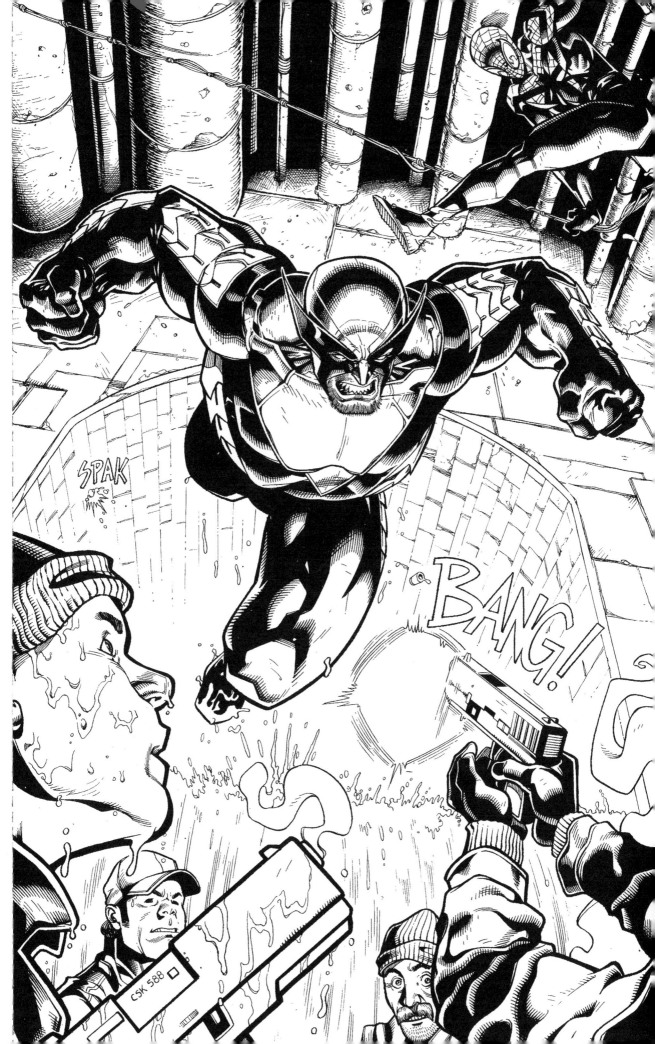

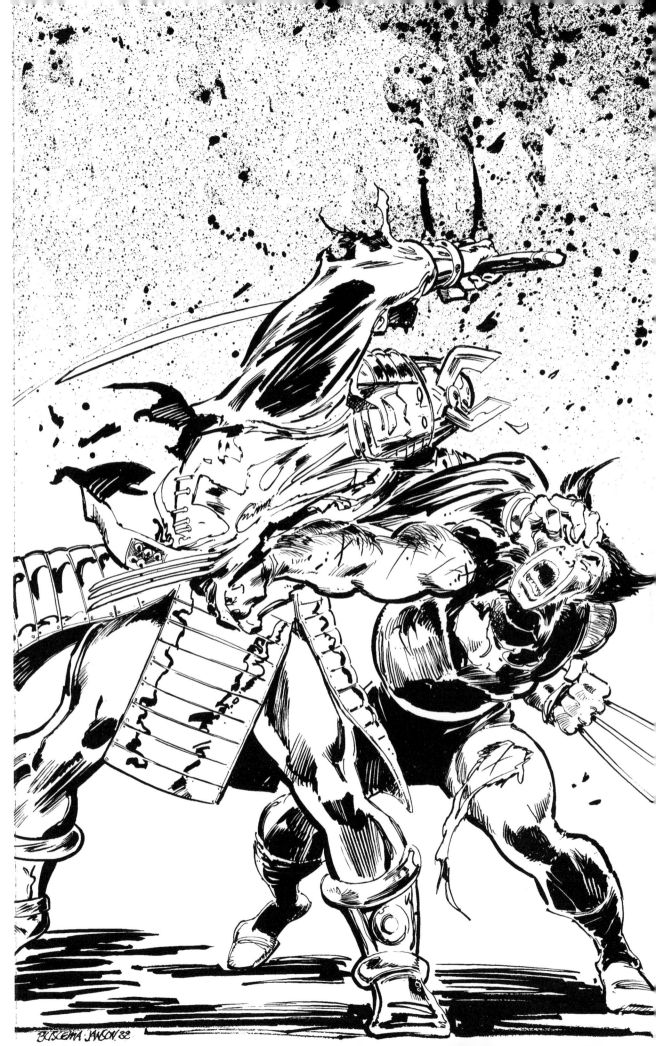

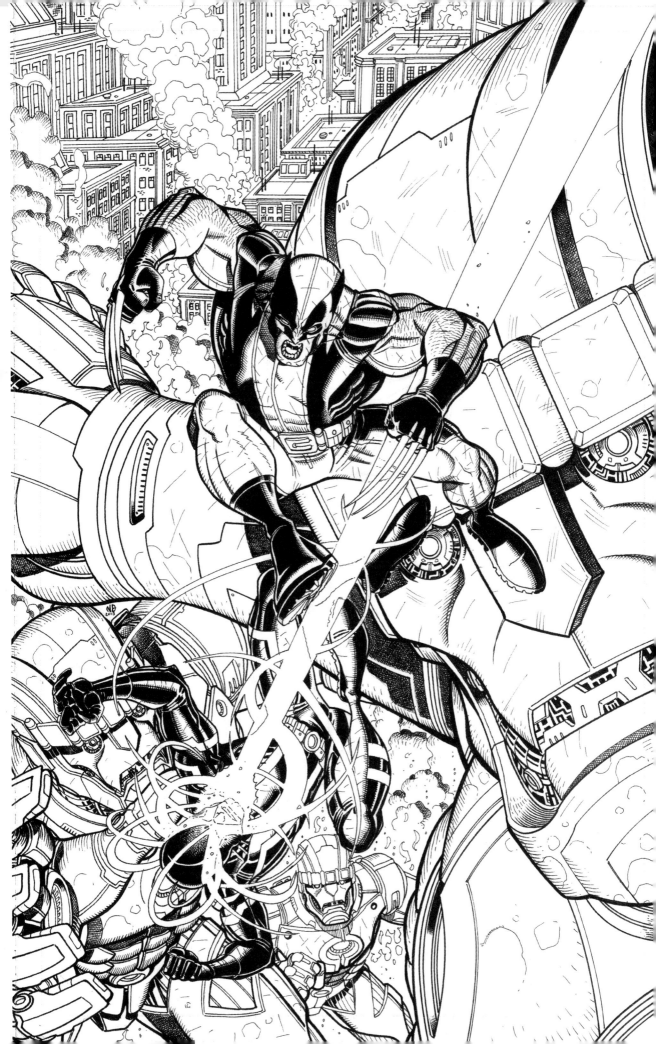

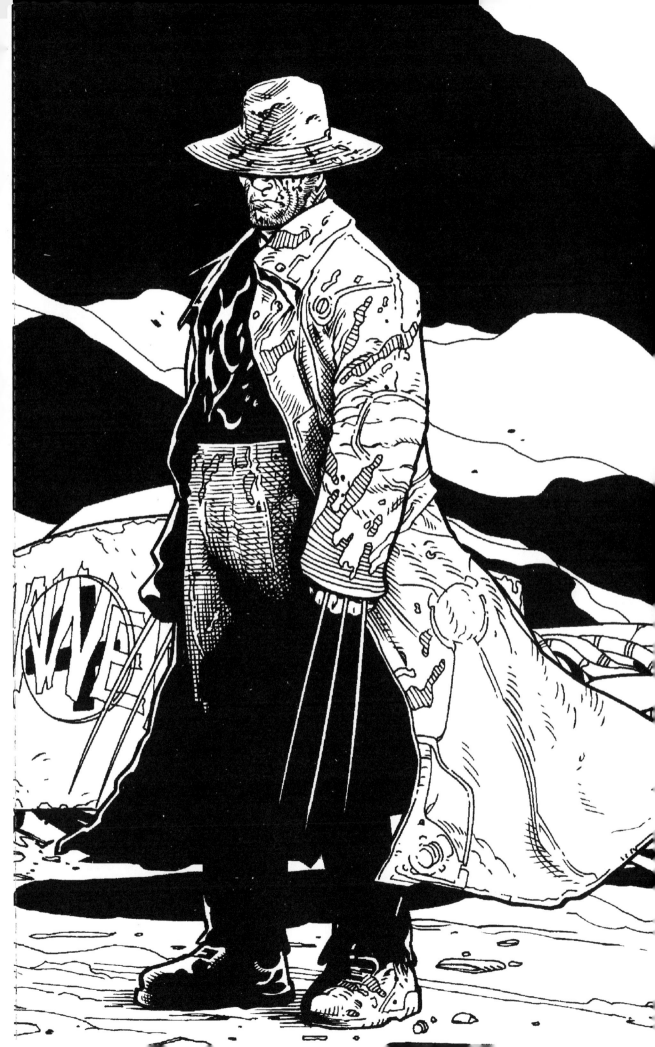

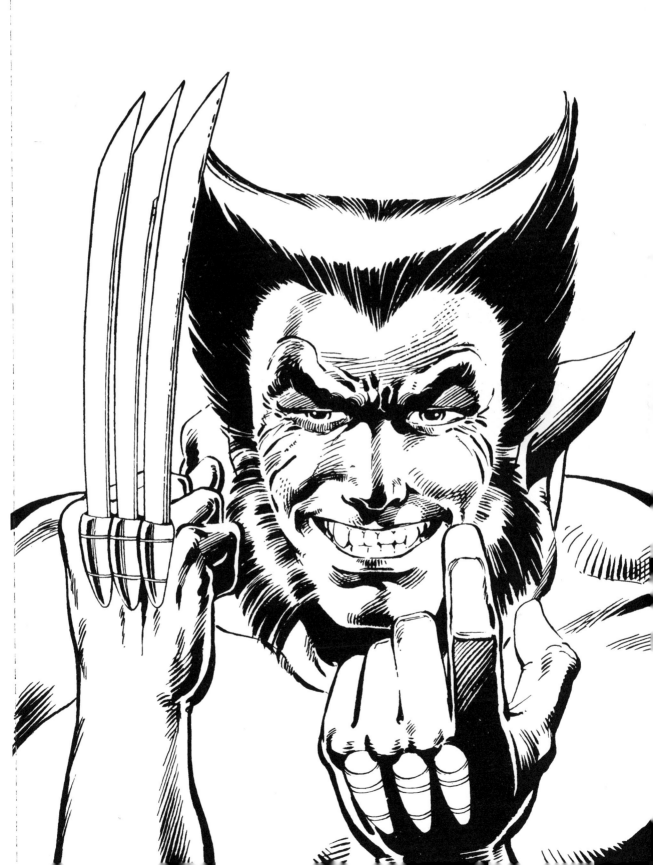

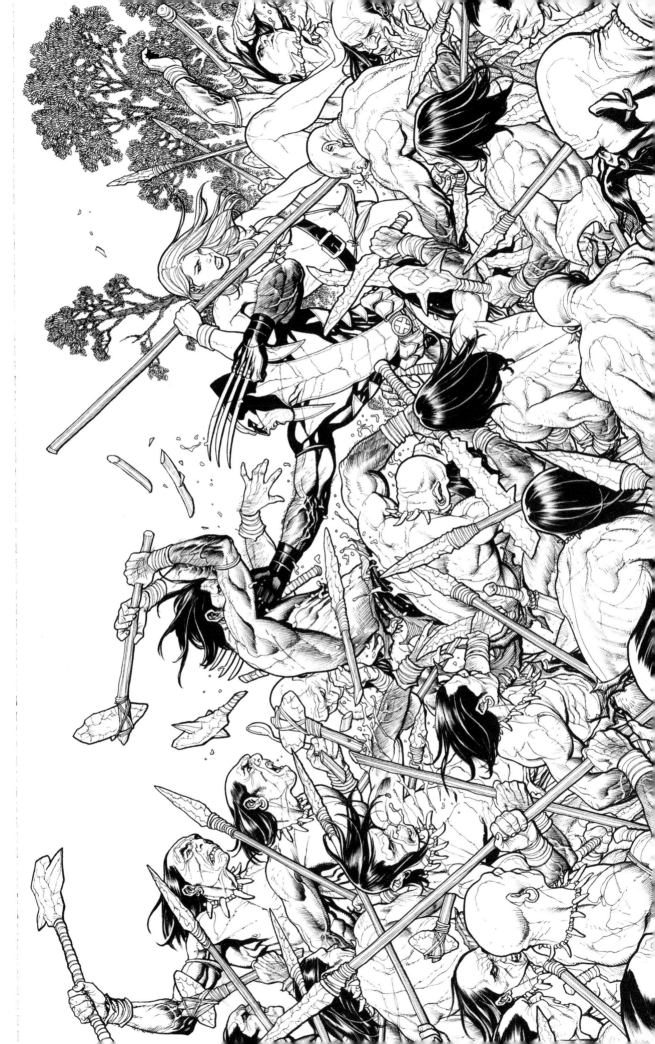

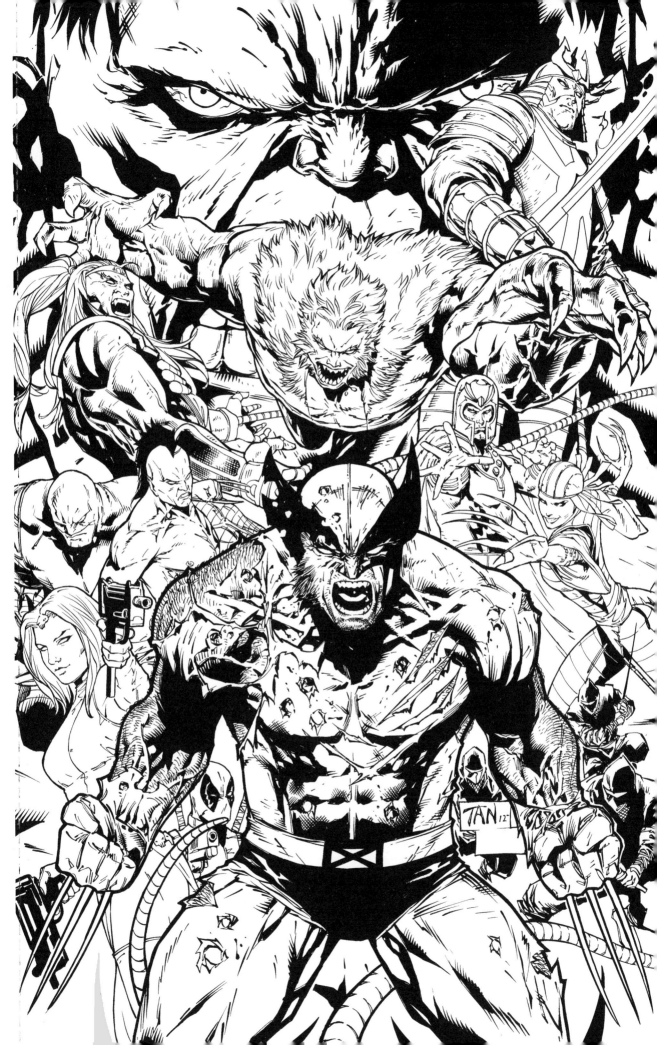

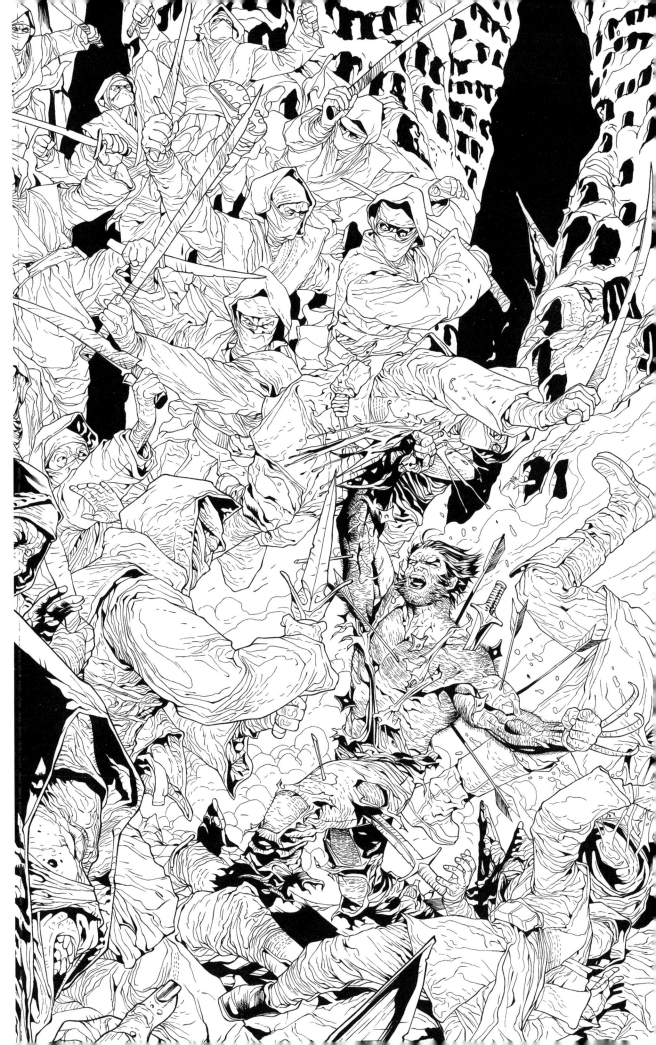

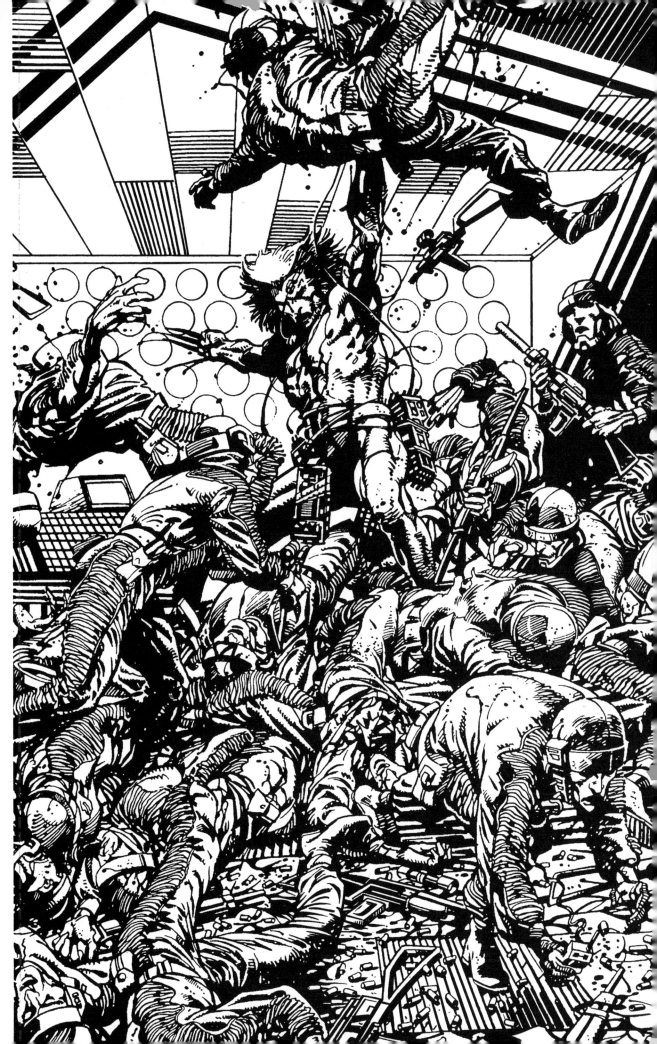

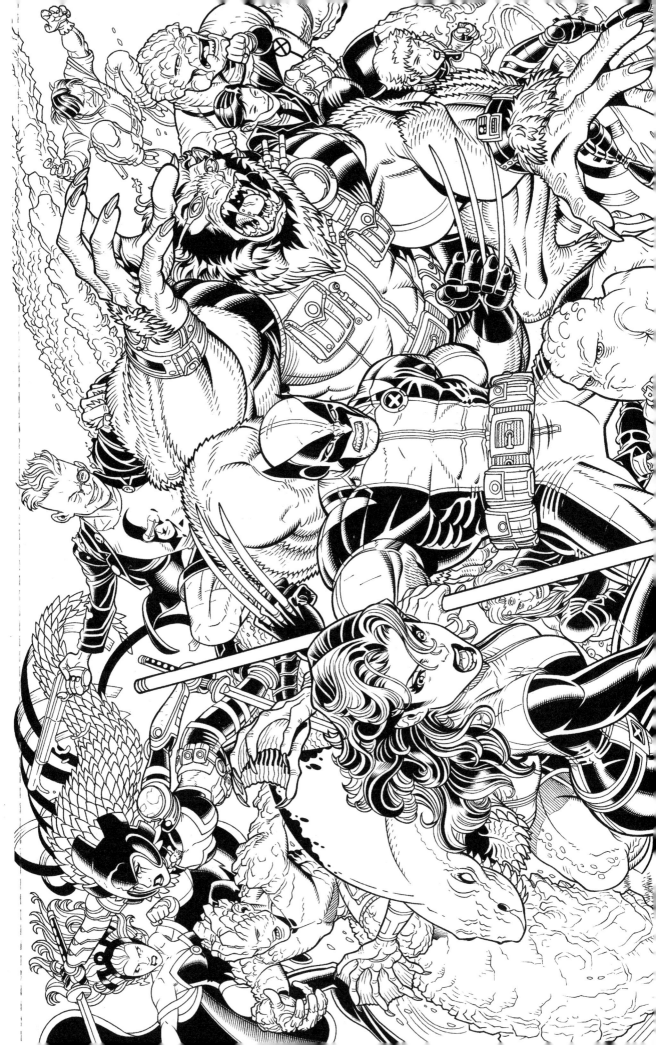

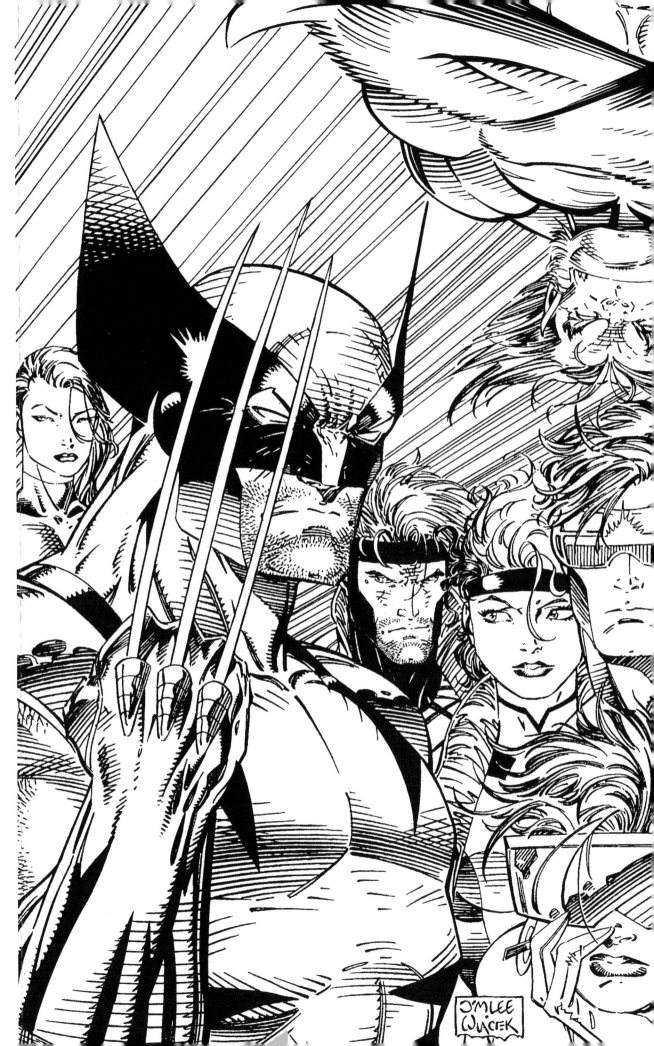

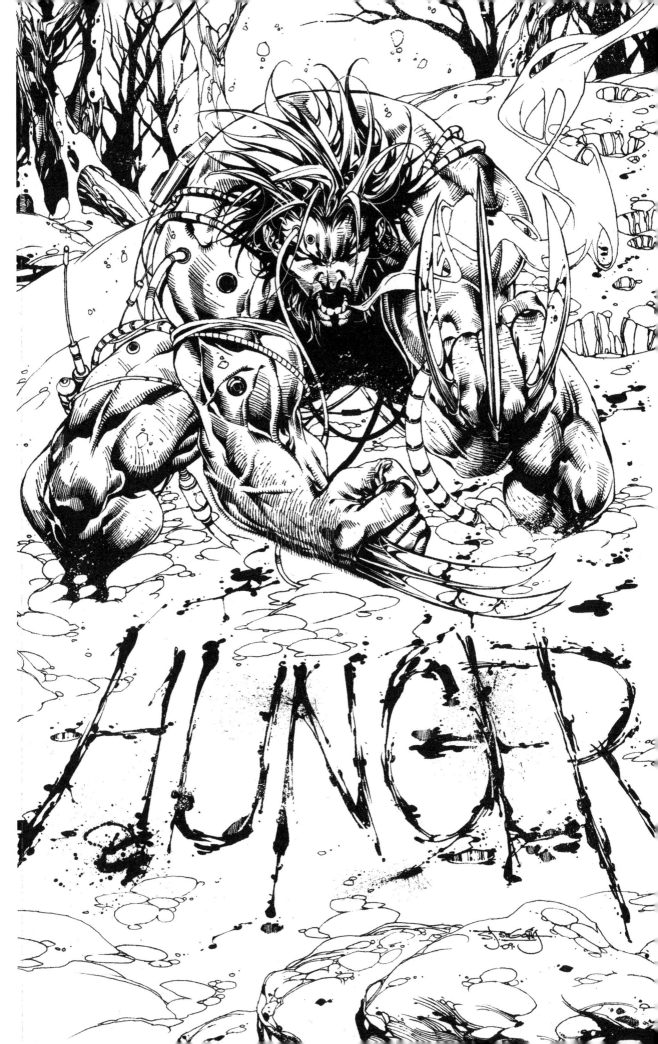

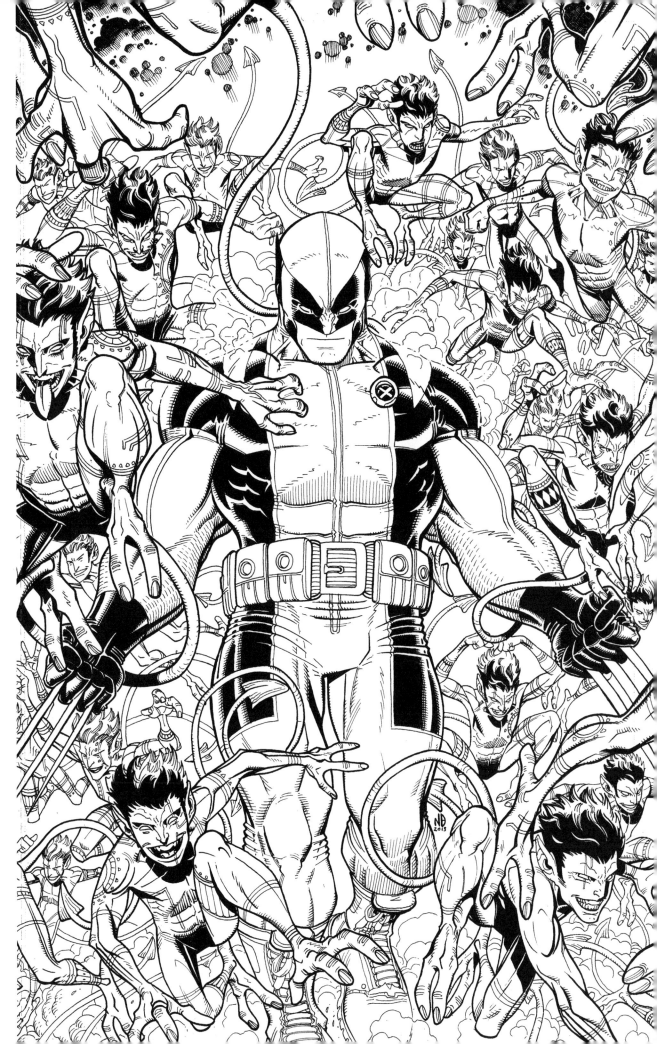

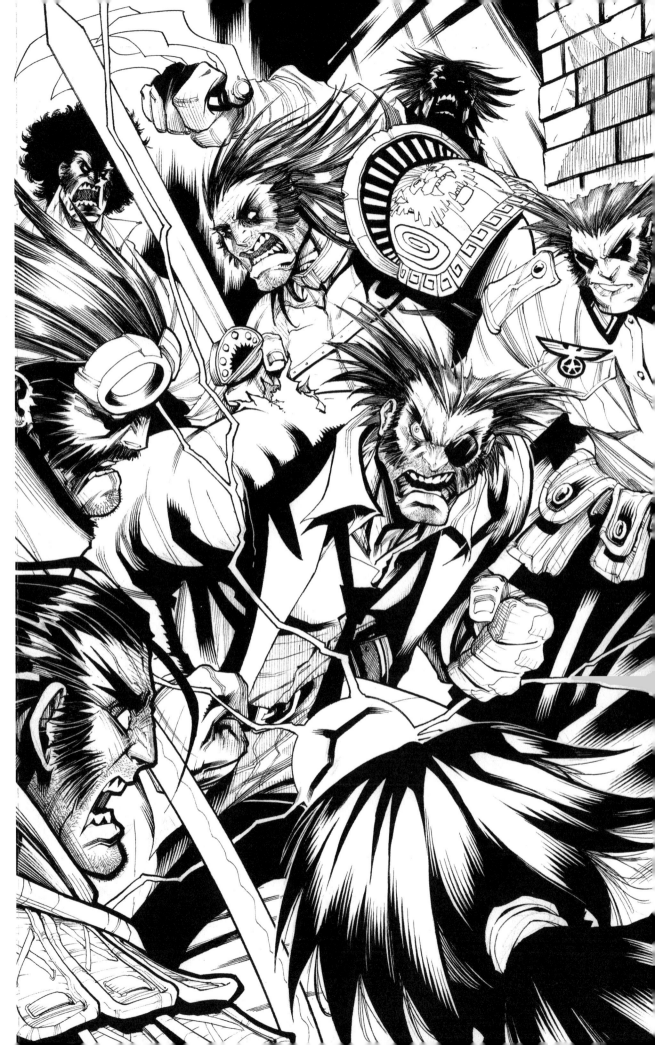

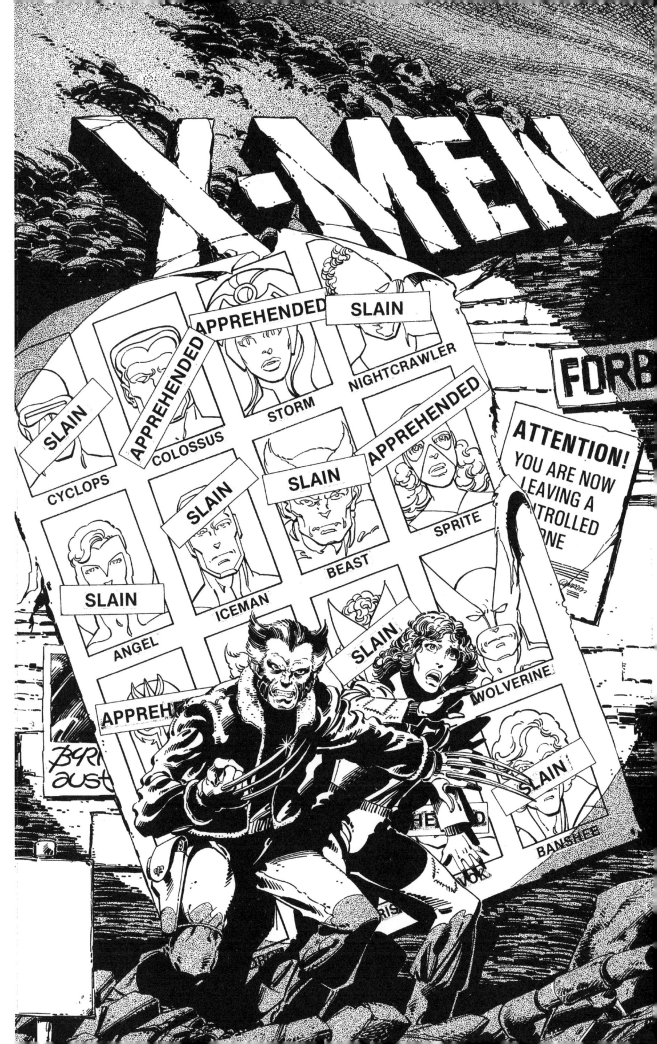

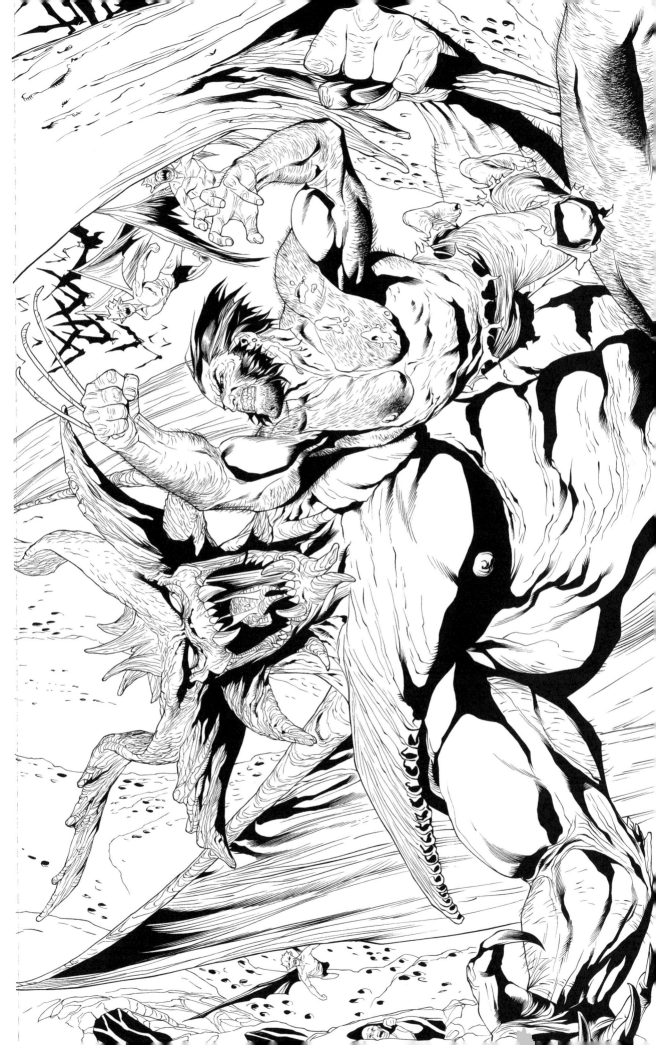

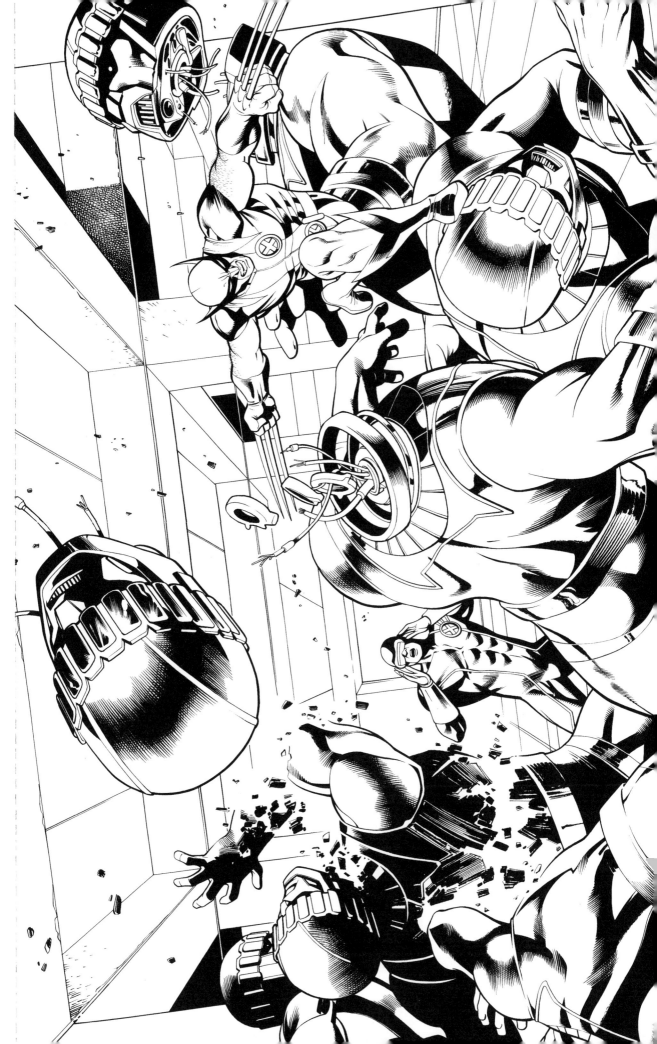

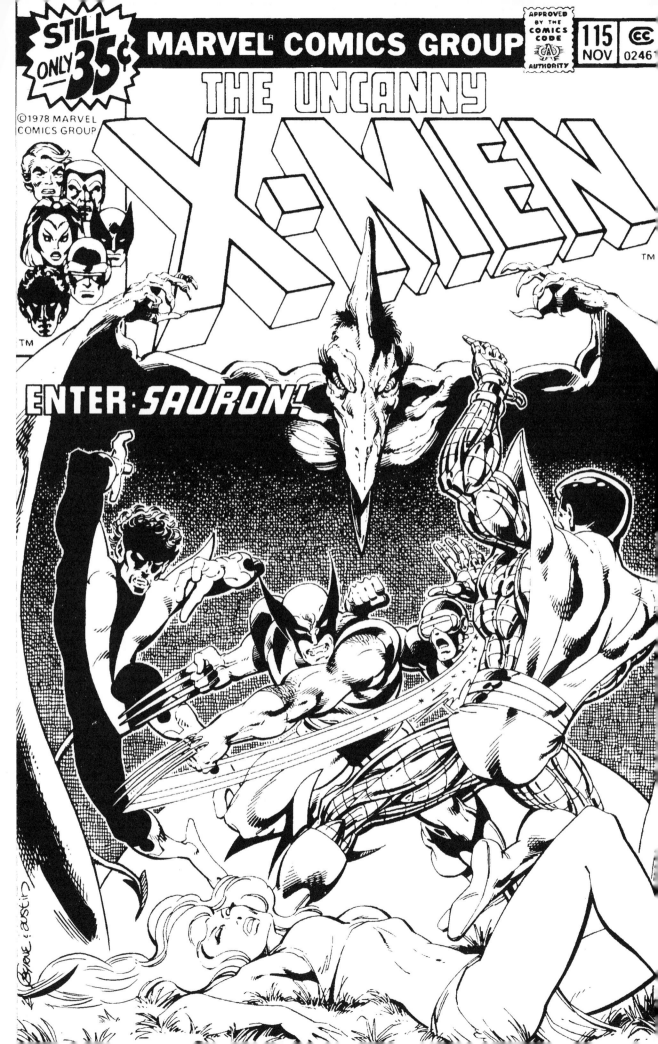

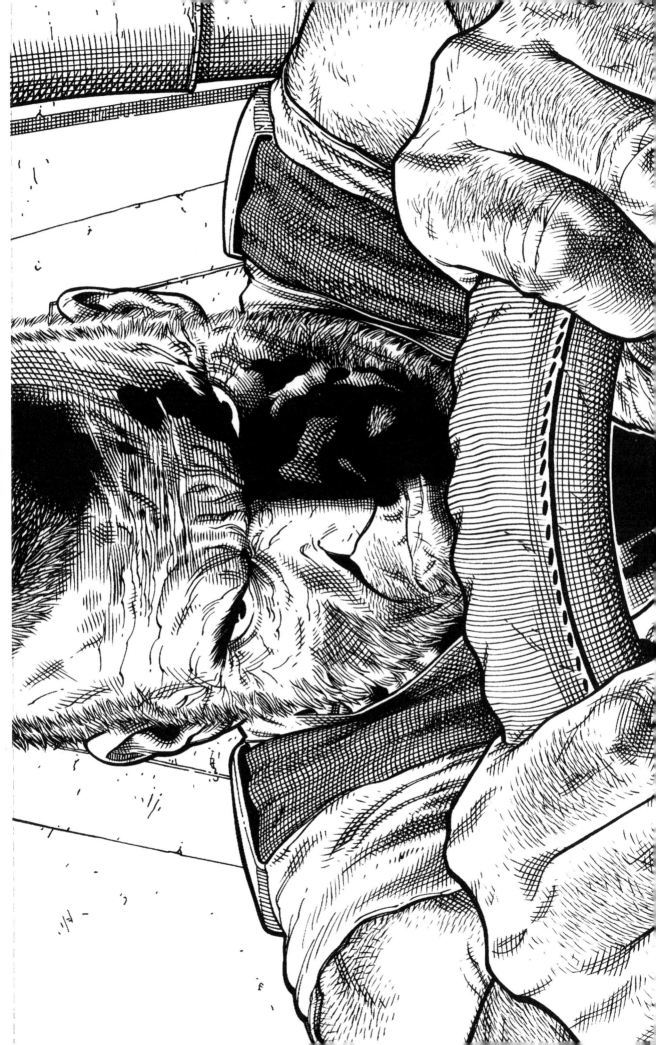

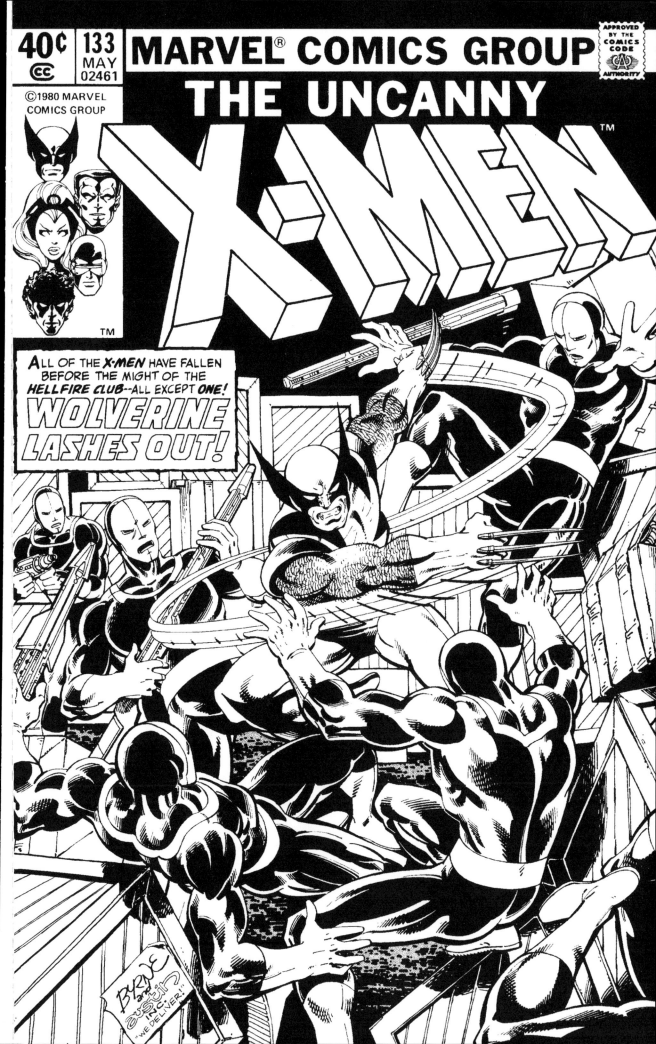

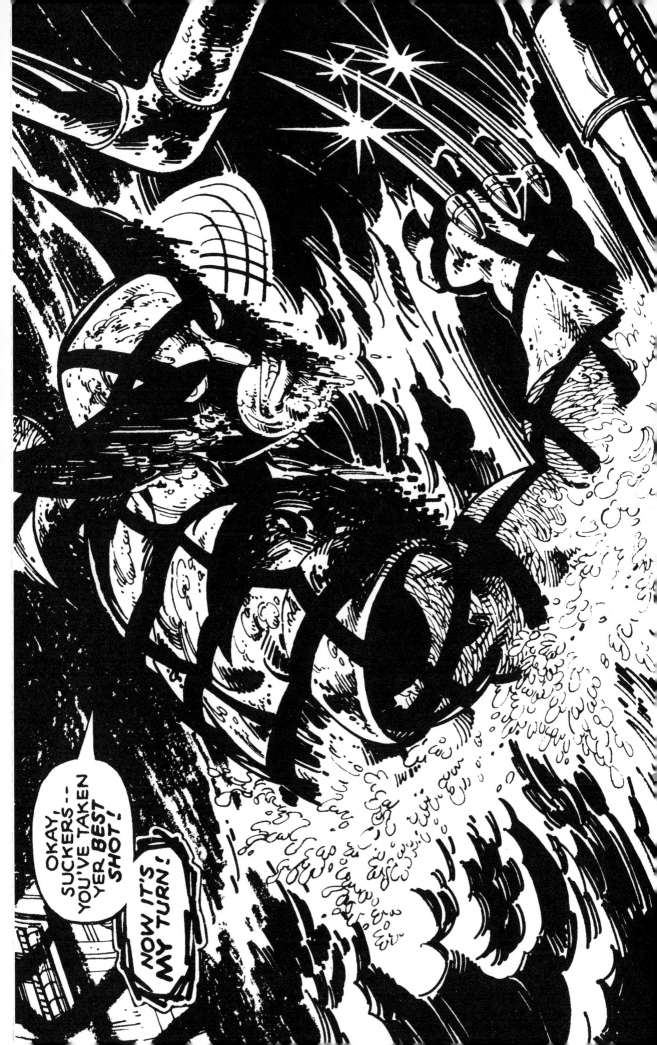

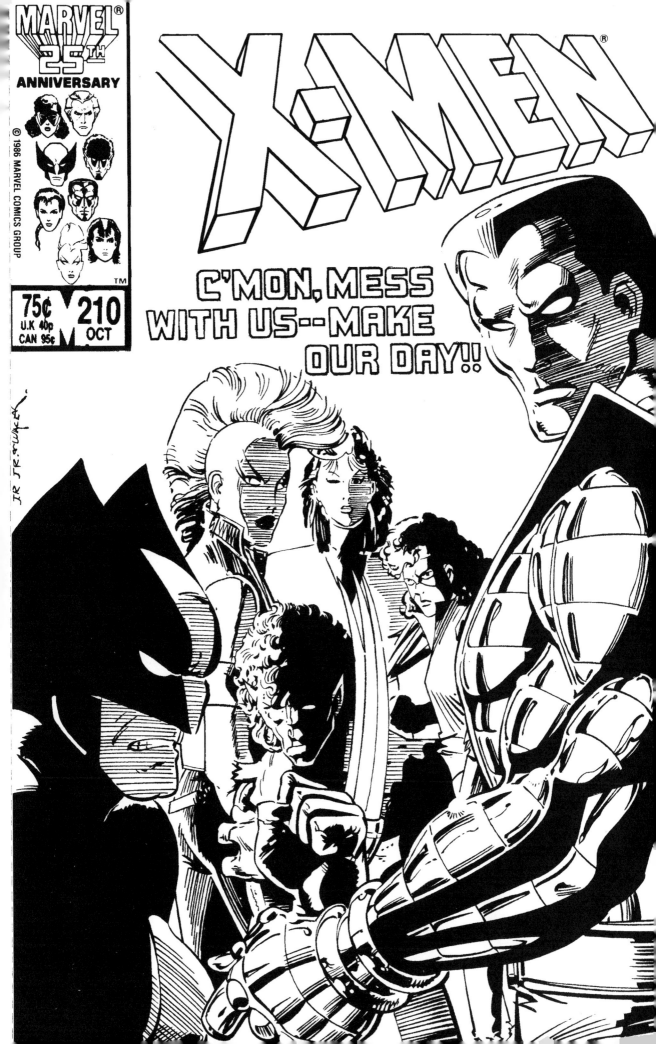